Pynchon's
Fictions

Pynchon's Fictions: Thomas Pynchon and the Literature of Information

JOHN O. STARK

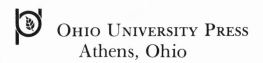

Ohio University Press
Athens, Ohio

© 1980 by John Stark
Printed in the United States of America
All rights reserved.

Library of Congress Cataloging in Publication Data

Stark, John O
    Pynchon's fictions.

    Includes bibliographical references.
    1. Pynchon, Thomas—Knowledge and learning.   2. Pynchon, Thomas—
Criticism and interpretation.
I. Title.
PS3566.Y55Z89   813'.54   79-28466
ISBN 0-8214-0419-9

This book is dedicated to Jeremy Stark

ACKNOWLEDGMENTS

For encouragement at crucial times during work on this book I am indebted to friends and former colleagues Louis Paskoff and Wayne Kvam. Professor Kvam also made many very useful editorial suggestions. I also thank my wife Faye and Jim Denton of the Ohio University Press for their help and Jan McInroy for her skillful copy-editing.

Contents

Introduction

During the spring of 1973 Thomas Pychon's *Gravity's Rainbow*, a huge novel, appeared. Its bulk, ambition, obscurity, and technical mastery made it much more than a book to be relegated to the "New and Novel" column in the *New York Times* and then forgotten. Pynchon's learning overwhelmed readers; he seemed to have ransacked entire libraries. Then, rather than strewing around bits of this information, he formed them into a coherent mosaic that gratified the reader's aesthetic faculties. Pynchon instantly became more than a coterie writer, a favorite of those who scribbled muted post horns on lavatory walls, imitated the Whole Sick Crew or, more sedately, used him to fill out yet another grouping of writers—the most frequent method of bringing order to current American fiction's disheveled state. The brief collection of critical studies on Pynchon grew slowly as some incisive and adulatory reviews were published. Pynchon attracted several major critics, such as Richard Poirier and Tony Tanner. Until now all his critics, however, although certainly not blind, have described only small parts of his most recent, elephantine book. Clearly *Gravity's Rainbow* demands a more thorough examination not only of itself but also of Pynchon's other works.

1

The traditional method of dividing literature into plot, character, structure, style, and the other elements does not suffice with Pynchon's work because he uses these elements in nontraditional ways. His books are made coherent in unusual ways. He also frequently refers to scientific information and theories, seeming to answer a charge made by C. P. Snow in *The Two Cultures and the Scientific Revolution*: "Once or twice I have been provoked and have asked the company how many of them could describe the Second Law of Thermodynamics. The response was cold: it was also negative. Yet I was asking something which is about the scientific equivalent of: *Have you read a work of Shakespeare's?*"[1] Pynchon shows not only that he understands the law of Clausius and the cyberneticists' adaptation of it, but also that he can integrate these ideas into a work of fiction, using them, for example, as metaphors. In other words, Pynchon seems to close the gap between the two cultures that alarmed Snow.

Pynchon's life gives few clues to his work; he is as private as Norman Mailer is public. But in spite of his allegiance to the tactics of silence, exile, and cunning, it is possible to compile a miniature biography of him. He was born in Glen Cove on Long Island on May 8, 1937, and he graduated from Cornell in 1958. While he attended Cornell novelistic excitement was bubbling beneath its lovely surface. Pynchon then knew a fellow student, Richard Fariña, who was to publish *Been Down So Long It Looks Like Up to Me* and later wrote a musical composition based on *V*. Pynchon dedicated *Gravity's Rainbow* to this friend, who died before his talent's full bloom. Moreover, Vladimir Nabokov still taught at Cornell. Although by the time of Pynchon's graduation Nabokov had published *Lolita, Pnin,* and many other books, most students remained oblivious to their teacher's eminence and knew him chiefly as the eccentric monarch of a course in modern literature that they called "Dirty Lit." Pynchon was a student in the course, and Vera Nabokov, who graded the examinations, recalls his work, mainly because his handwriting was half printing, half longhand. Characteristically, at this time his interests encompassed both literature and science. While at Cornell he wrote a few stories that were later published. After interrupting his studies for two years in the navy, Pynchon graduated from Cornell in 1958. Then he moved toward the literary pole of his interests, declining a Woodrow Wilson Fellowship in favor of living in Greenwich Village for a year. Next he reversed directions and obtained a job with Boeing, learning technical information that he later used in *Gravity's Rainbow*.

His career turned again when he went to Mexico to finish *V.*, which received considerable acclaim and won the William Faulkner First Novel Award. From then on he has lived by his pen and inside his own mind, preferring to remain unnoticed and unavailable. In addition to his fairly well-known works—*V.* (1960), *The Crying of Lot 49* (1963), and "Entropy" (1960)—his early writing includes portions of *V.* published as short stories, "Low-lands" (a story for *New World Writing*), "Mortality and Mercy in Vienna" (his first story), "The Secret Integration" (which appeared in *Saturday Evening Post*), and "Journey into the Mind of Watts" (reportage for the *New York Times* that is impressive for its empathy).

Because it requires finding order in apparent chaos, an exhaustive analysis of Pynchon's work is much more difficult than assembling biographical data about him. One can discern a grand design that organizes all its obscure parts, however, if one visualizes his work as three concentric circles. The inner circle, the texture, represents Pynchon's description of unmediated everyday reality. That is, in the elements of his fiction he presents the confusion that vexes people who have no ordering principle to make details fit together to help them discover meanings. The first chapter of this study shows how the elements of Pynchon's fiction, by disputing common sense and flouting the conventions of realistic fiction, produce chaos. His writing, as George Levine claims, "challenges fundamental, usually unspoken literary and cultural assumptions."[2] At this point the world and the mirror of literature are both cracked, and chaos is compounded.

The middle five chapters of this study describe the second of the concentric circles by examining the information that Pynchon borrows from science and technology, psychology, history, religion, and the film. The second part of each of these chapters explains Pynchon's references to the methods of organizing information employed by these disciplines. He concentrates on one scientific law (the Second Law of Thermodynamics), on scientific epistemology's hypothesis that cause-and-effect relationships exist, on two scientific disciplines that can synthesize information from various branches of science (mathematics and cybernetics), on several schools of psychology, on theories of historical causation, on two religious world views and on theories of the film's nature and functions. Explaining both information from and theories about each discipline goes a long way toward illuminating Pynchon's work. However, all of these disciplines fail to organize satisfactorily the enormous amount of information available to contemporary people. Although this task is probably hopeless, Pynchon's literature can be understood as an effort to work toward its accomplishment. The last chapter of this study turns to his literary allusions and his analysis of the nature of literature, and the last of the three concentric circles consists of his own literary uses of information.

1.

The Elements of Fiction

While creating his plots Pynchon works against a background of traditional effort to connect by means of intricate causal relations a series of significant actions. Recent novelists have of course often abandoned this effort in favor of randomness, which reached its ultimate stage with the cutout novel that a reader can assemble in any order. Pynchon handles plot with particular skill in *The Crying of Lot 49*, where every action counts. *Gravity's Rainbow* and *V.* have equally ingenious but very different kinds of plots, in which intricacies multiply seemingly without limit, but order, albeit of an unfamiliar kind, does exist.

Most noticeably, Pynchon makes improbable the individual events he describes. For example, the adenoid that runs loose in the early pages of *Gravity's Rainbow* does not accord with everyday reality, or even with the rest of that bizarre scene.[1] Similarly, later in the same novel Pynchon describes a schizophrenic who thinks he is World War II. On this scaffolding of the barely possible the author builds a superstructure of impossibility: this man's physical condition varies with the progress of the war. For example, the Normandy landing raises his temperature. Another impossibility is that Slothrop's sexual activities, when marked on a map of London, predict the places where German rockets will fall. George Levine explains the

5

effects of such improbable events and of other common features of Pynchon's work: "Pynchon's novels disorient. They offer us a world we think we recognize, assimilate it to worlds that seem unreal, imply coherences and significances we can't quite hold on to. Invariably, as the surreal takes on the immediacy of experience, they make us feel the inadequacy of conventional modes of making sense—of analysis, causal explanation, logic."[2]

Pynchon also casts doubt on common preconceptions by describing events that both are credible in themselves and reflect another realm of being. For example, three characters in *Gravity's Rainbow*, though a bit strange, fall within the limits of the willing suspension of disbelief. In their attempt to escape the war, however, "Katje, Gottfried, and Captain Blicero have agreed that this Northern and ancient form, one they all know and are comfortable with—the strayed children, the wood-wife in the edible house, the captivity, the fattening, the Oven—shall be their preserving routine, their shelter, against what outside none of them can bear—the War, the absolute rule of chance, their own pitiable contingency here, in its midst" (p. 96). In other words, in addition to being at least somewhat realistic characters, as their response to the war shows, they reenact the fairy tale of Hansel and Gretel. This retelling of the legend, especially the prominence given to the oven, forms an analogy with the holocaust and recalls the rocket's engine. Realistic fiction, folklore, and history merge, further shaking the reader's willingness to believe that the plot could happen.

To balance the unreal aspects of the plot of *Gravity's Rainbow*, Pynchon often refers to the war's historical actuality. In fact, he somehow has discovered countless minute details about life in wartime London. The events of the war chronicled in history books appear in this novel mainly by inference, as Pynchon attends to this other kind of information. The extent of his research is evident in passages like this one: "With a mortar and pestle he pulverizes the substance and dumps it into an old Huntley & Palmers biscuit tin, reserving only enough to roll deftly up in a Rizla liquorice cigarette paper, light, and inhale the smoke of" (p. 93). His uncomfortably exact reproduction of Southern California in *The Crying of Lot 49* shows a similar attention to detail. A reader can react to this mixture of the undeniably real and the incredible by extending his or her belief to that which was previously unbelieved, thereby choosing to trust for accurate reports of reality anyone who knows about such obscurities as Huntley & Palmers biscuits. More likely, because Pynchon creates so much confusion by mixing kinds of reality, a reader will begin to doubt some of his or her own certainties.

To produce further skepticism Pynchon employs the technique of infinite regress. At one point in *Gravity's Rainbow* a scientist who drives rats through a maze realizes that the laboratory itself is a maze in which the humans respond as the rats do (p. 229). This laboratory plays a prominent role in *Gravity's Rainbow* but after the scientist's realization it does not appear to be real, or at least not real in the same way it had seemed. That is, the lab's ontological status apparently changes. The technique of infinite regressions has traditionally been a method of refutation but, more important, multiplying kinds of reality in this way implies that independent entities do not exist in any simple sense. That is, something may be real from the perspective of one realm, but not from that of another. Pynchon thus disputes a belief crucial to common sense—that entities are distinct and independent.

In addition to making individual details seem unreal, Pynchon also disturbs conventional notions of reality by frequently suggesting that the author made the plot out of nothing rather than by connecting actions as they are connected in the real world. The intricate plots of his two long novels provide obvious examples, and, although he uses a different method in *The Crying of Lot 49*, Pynchon also forces its reader to recognize the plot's intricacy. He inserts a plot summary of *The Courier's Tragedy*, a play that some of the characters perform (p. 45 ff.). This pseudo-Jacobean play has an incredibly complex plot; a summary of it, with a few brief interpolations, runs for eight pages. Pynchon creates here more than the necessary intricacy, which suggests that Pynchon, rather than events, controls the plot.

Pynchon accomplishes the same effect by describing many more coincidences than an imitation of everyday reality would allow. For example, characters who have careened in and out of the plot but have remained separate suddenly meet. In *V.* when Kurt Mondaugen stands on a balcony in Southwest Africa, Hugh Godolphin suddenly appears next to him. In the same book the lives of Herbert Stencil and Benny Profane usually remain separate, but late in the novel Stencil goes to Malta to search for the mysterious V. A priest there tells him about his predecessor, Father Fairing, about whom Profane had heard because Fairing had tried to convert the rats in the same sewers in which Profane hunted alligators. In *The Crying of Lot 49* the main character, Oedipa Maas, unlike most of the characters in *V.*, recognizes that a web of coincidence is being woven around her. Or does this web exist of its own accord? Or does it not exist after all? Pynchon uses her experiences with muted post horns, postal systems, and Pierce Inverarity's empire to insinuate dozens of coincidences into his novel. In addition to those that connect details within the fictional realm of the book, a few connect details in the main story line to the play within the novel, as a character recognizes: " '*The Courier's Tragedy*,' said Miles, 'she's right. The same kind of kinky thing, you know. Bones of lost battalion in lake, fished up, turned into charcoal' " (p. 43). *Gravity's Rainbow* also has numerous coincidences of both kinds. With more subplots and episodes than *V.*, it even more frequently than the earlier novel has characters from different plot lines suddenly coming together. Here, too, coincidences link seemingly distinct levels of reality. At one point some of the characters attend a pantomime of Hansel and Gretel, which three characters reenact elsewhere. In this novel Pynchon also interrelates events to form coincidences. For example, the harmonica that falls down the toilet at the Roseland Ball Room in Boston early in the novel turns up much later in a European pastoral setting. Pynchon exercises amazing control over these effects.

Such coincidences reinforce the theme of paranoia that runs through all his books, especially *Gravity's Rainbow*. After the characters recognize a few coincidences, they begin to see a threatening order in them. Finally they change their minds and begin to doubt that they can understand events at all. At this point Pynchon suggests that the characters had merely imagined the order that they thought existed. Their rage for order eventually expands to paranoid proportions. Pynchon does not create order because he wishes to show his characters' paranoia. More certainly, he does not create order because he is paranoid himself—a charge, often veiled, sometimes relatively open, that some critics have made. Rather, he manipulates coincidences and the motif of paranoia to call attention to the much more useful and satisfying ordering activity of the literary artist.

Finally, Pynchon's plots rebut belief in cause and effect. The inability of the characters to understand, much less control, cause-and-effect relationships continually thwarts them and even contributes to the paranoia of some of them. Other characters react aimlessly to their lack of control over their own lives. Most vividly, the rocket attacks on London described in *Gravity's Rainbow*, frightening enough because the inhabitants cannot stop them, become almost unbearable when supersonic rockets begin to fall, because they strike before they are heard, which further scrambles cause and effect.

His plots as wholes also argue against the existence of cause-and-effect relations. Their endings, which do not result from and thereby make sense of all the earlier causes, are particularly effective attacks on cause-and-effect analysis. *V.* ends with the death of Herbert Stencil's father, which Pynchon has also recounted many pages earlier. The final version, although precise and striking, adds no valuable information for either Herbert or the reader. On the contrary, it underscores Herbert's confusion. If his father were still alive, he would be able to provide some clues about the puzzle of V., which dominates Herbert's existence. The ending of *The Crying of Lot 49* seems more like a prologue. The final two sentences, whose effect typifies that of Pynchon's plots, are "The auctioneer cleared his throat. Oedipa settled back, to await the crying of lot 49" (p. 138). Nothing follows this preparatory throat clearing; the mystery of Pierce Inverarity and the alternative postal system, perhaps answered in part (lot 49) of this stamp collection, remains as murky as ever. In fact, the inconclusive ending emphasizes that murkiness. Whereas methods of analysis based on a belief in causality cannot account for the conclusion, understanding Pynchon's unusual methods of organizing literary material may make an explanation of it possible. *Gravity's Rainbow* concludes with a hymn to be sung by an imaginary movie audience as it watches the bouncing ball on the screen. The hymn describes a set of events apocalyptic in its finality but not in its obfuscation. Enigmatic abstractions and a mixture of imagery, for instance from Puritan theology and World War II, cause some of the confusion. The final passage reads:

> There is a Hand to turn the time,
> Though thy Glass today be run,
> Till the Light that hath brought the Towers low
> Find the last poor Pret'rite one . . .
> Till the Riders sleep by ev'ry road,
> All through our crippl'd Zone,
> With a face on ev'ry mountainside,
> And a Soul in ev'ry stone. . . .
>
> Now everybody— (p. 760).

Strange joints hold together the structures of these novels. Often a transition will call into question the credibility of the next passage. In *V.*, one section ends "He'd only the veiled references to Porpentine in the journals. The rest was impersonation and dream" (p. 52). This invitation to skepticism is followed by a meticulous description of an adventure of Porpentine, in which the multiple points of view support rather than negate each other, adding credibility to the episode. Nevertheless, because his monomania distorts everything he experiences, if Stencil has dreamed, this account is not to be believed. Furthermore, although not an important consideration, the adventure appeared separately as "Under the Rose."[3] Readers who realize this will probably wonder about the episode's relation to the rest of the plot.

In other places Pynchon juxtaposes incidents rather than welding them together. Sometimes an obvious similarity causes two incidents to resonate with each other. For example, one part of *V.* ends with Esther's leaving her plastic surgeon's home after having sex with him. It shows that he has turned her into an object both psychologically, by his attitude toward her, and literally, by performing surgery on her. The succeeding episode presents SHROUD as an almost human object that symbolizes the semihumanity of many of the characters. This description of SHROUD also develops the novel's social dimension, which includes stories about exploiters who turn large groups of people, such as the African Hereros, into objects. Even such a subtle connection happens infrequently in Pynchon's work. More often, episodes have no apparent connection to each other, and sometimes a time shift further complicates matters. In *The Crying of Lot 49*, however, the action does move forward in an orderly time sequence, which creates some coherence. And Scott Simmon has pointed out a clever, unusual ordering principle in *Gravity's Rainbow*: "To have the characters and the narrative consciousness see ostensibly diverse episodes united into a single plot provides the novel with a unity it could not otherwise possess."[4]

Critics have responded in two contrasting ways to Pynchon's structures. Richard Locke illustrates one position: "In *Gravity's Rainbow* the structure is strained beyond the breaking point. Reading it is often profoundly exasperating."[5] In contrast, Tony Tanner more convincingly says of *V.*, "Pynchon is able to explore the plot-making instinct itself. To this end his own novel has to appear to be relatively unplotted—leaving chunks of data around, as it were, for Stencil to try to interrelate."[6] Tanner rightly identifies a major purpose of Pynchon's loose structures, although the plot-making instinct motivates Pynchon himself much more significantly than it motivates his characters. With this one amendment Tanner's judgment goes to the heart of Pynchon's enterprise, showing the great importance of information and its assimilation to his short stories and novels.

Plot making thus ties together Pynchon's novels. The efforts of the characters to fit things together into patterns constantly recapitulate Pynchon's grand plot making. The characters also work fervently to solve epistemological puzzles in these novels, which, unlike most, emphasize such intellectual tasks. Other similarities also knot together his plots. Characters repeatedly stand alone, or with the support of one other character, against a mass of people or the weight of events. Also, each novel tells the story of the main character's quest: in *V.* Stencil searches for V; in *The Crying of Lot 49* Oedipa seeks to understand Inverarity's estate and to determine whether or not the Tristero exists; in *Gravity's Rainbow* Tyrone Slothrop searches for the rocket. Minor characters also seek things. For example, many characters in *Gravity's Rainbow* try to find the same rocket, and Paola Maijstral in *V.* looks for her husband. These common endeavors make Pynchon's plots somewhat orderly, but they leave loose ends so that he can dramatize plot making.

The names of the characters also reveal that Pynchon uses them in strange ways. Many of the names both provoke laughter and reveal the character's personality. Several contemporary writers, such as J. P. Donleavy, use this technique. The names of Richard Fariña's characters, however, most closely resemble Pynchon's. Many characters in *Been Down So Long It Looks Like Up to Me*, such as Gnossos, have names like those in Pynchon's novels. Fariña's novel appeared in 1966, as did *The Crying of Lot 49*, and Pynchon had already created such names in *V.* If influence exists, Pynchon probably deserves the credit. However, his stay at Cornell, like the rest of his life, is an enigma; he and Fariña could very well have jointly worked out this fictional strategy or learned it from someone else.

A few of Pynchon's characters, such as Genghis Cohen, the philatelist in *The Crying of Lot 49*, have allusive or otherwise revealing names. Besides its small joke, Cohen's name suggests the mysterious threat he poses to Oedipa. Others have foreign names that suit them. The plastic surgeon in *V.* is named Schoenmaker ("beautiful maker," which turns out to be ironic). A sybarite is called Zeitsuss ("sweet time"), and Weissmann ("white man") is a death figure and searcher for a Black named Enzian. Some of the English names also convert easily into meanings: Dewey Gland, Herbert Stencil (who sees the pattern of V. in everything), and Roger Pointsman. The author himself in *Gravity's Rainbow* explains the last of these examples: "He is the pointsman. He is called that because he throws the lever that changes the points" (p. 644). In other words, this man with a name that means a railroad switchman controls the movements of others.

Some characters have names with obvious significance but far from obvious meaning. Does "Rachel Owlglass" suggest wisdom and the vanity of a mirror gazer, or wisdom and the brittleness of glass, or something else? Pierce Inverarity, the mystery man of *The Crying of Lot 49*, has an appropriately ambiguous last name. David K. Kirby contends that changing one letter produces " 'inveracity,' and the name becomes a powerful imperative: to penetrate the lie."[7] His analysis, however, requires considering Inverarity to be an oracle, which the novel's plot does not justify. Moreover, the inveracities that need piercing remain unspecified. Joseph W. Slade points out that Inverarity, Scotland, was a bastion of the Protestant Reformation and that Pynchon may be implying that Weber was correct about the relationship between Protestantism and capitalism.[8] Most convincingly, Richard Poirier remarks that there is a stamp dealer named Pierce and that the stamps in this novel are "inverse rarities."[9] The name of Tyrone Slothrop, the most important character in *Gravity's Rainbow*, presents great difficulties. W. T. Lhamon, Jr., argues that this name combines "sloth" and "ROP," "the term used when an editor has the right to place an ad wherever is convenient in a paper."[10] Although the second part of this interpretation makes some sense—despite Slothrop's free movements and those determined by his search for the rocket—the first part ascribes to him a quality that he does not exhibit. Also, Pynchon used this name earlier for a character in "The Secret Integration."[11] The name Oedipa Maas immediately stimulates associations. Kirby argues that the riddle solving of Oedipus applies here, but a reader will inevitably remember other parts of the myth and its psychoanalytic meanings, some of which do not apply to Oedipa (Kirby, p. 388). Pynchon may be trying to blur rather than sharpen this character's outlines, making the point not one among many natural associations but confusion itself.

James Dean Young more convincingly explains these four ambiguous names and many others. In Pynchon's fiction, Young writes, "the device of naming characters significantly turns out to be that of giving them meanings which they do not have or do not develop or about which we cannot judge."[12] His generalization covers a bit too much ground since it does not apply to all the characters, but it fits many of them and also is consistent with Pynchon's efforts to discredit common sense by showing that things cannot be understood as easily as some people imagine.

Despite the similar effects of their names, Oedipa and Slothrop differ significantly in one of the functions that characters may serve. Oedipa, a protagonist, focuses the action, and as a result of it changes from a stereotypical Southern California housewife to a woman of almost tragic stature searching for truths large and small and for human contact. This traditional use of a character helps to make *The Crying of Lot 49* easier to comprehend than the other novels. Slothrop, however, has only slightly more importance than other characters. The tumultuous action of *Gravity's Rainbow* often leaves him behind; in fact, he virtually has disappeared by the novel's end. Also, although his knowledge grows, he remains implacable in the face of all the things that could teach and influence him. Hopelessness, not strength of character, induces his constancy, which implies one of this novel's bleak messages. In *V.* Herbert Stencil, Benny Profane, and perhaps others contend for the role of protagonist, and it is difficult to distinguish Benny from his compatriots. Like *Gravity's Rainbow*, *V.* has characters who change little or not at all, although apparently some change occurs, since as the novel progresses information about the characters accumulates. Pynchon, then, eschews some traditional ways of delineating characters.

As he sketches his characters, Pynchon attacks several commonsense notions about people: that they are three-dimensional, have a unique identity, remain fairly consistent, are understandable, and have reasonably unified personalities despite their complexities. Pynchon's creation of many stereotyped rather than three-dimensional characters needs little documentation. For instance, Benny Profane is a schlemiel, as a typical account of his actions indicates: "The water came out hot and cold in random patterns. He danced around, yowling and shivering, slipped on a bar of soap and nearly broke his neck. Drying off, he ripped a frayed towel in half, rendering it useless. He put on his skivvy shirt backwards, took ten minutes getting his fly zipped and another fifteen repairing a shoelace which had broken as he was tying it" (p. 27). On he wanders through disaster after misfortune after faux pas. Rachel's claim that he is not a schlemiel convinces neither him nor me but, in case anyone has missed it, points out the stereotype that he fits (p. 360).

Pynchon attacks more subtly the concept of personal identity. Sometimes a character, probably speaking for his creator, tries to refute it. In *The Crying of Lot 49* Oedipa's husband claims, " 'Everybody who says the same words is the same person if the spectra are the same only they happen differently in time' " (p. 106). A radio announcer, he phrases his attack on this concept in electronic terms. In *Gravity's Rainbow* Laszlo Jamf states a theory of human personality that makes everyone basically identical: " '[There is] a lion in each one of you. He is either tamed—by too much mathematics, by details of design, by corporate procedures—or he stays wild, an eternal predator' " (p. 577). These and other theories held by characters would be unconvincing if they were not reinforced by the techniques Pynchon uses to construct characters. For example, his repeated use of disguises counsels skepticism about identity. At times his novels read like Shakespeare's early comedies, their characters entering in various human and even nonhuman disguises, switching disguises, masking and unmasking. Pynchon, however, builds a macabre backdrop for this festivity. For example, in *Gravity's Rainbow* Major Marvy assumes at the wrong moment Slothrop's disguise of Plechazunga, a pig-hero, and pays for his bad timing with castration, an operation described in more than Jacobean goriness. Raymond Olderman points out another trait of Pynchon's that has the same effect on conventional beliefs about character. "German names and German characters," he writes, "constantly appear in connection with ominous intimations."[13] In other words, Pynchon makes Germans seem nearly interchangeable; they all foretell disaster. Olderman cites five examples from *V.*, and many more could be drawn from *Gravity's Rainbow*.

In addition to Oedipa Maas, some of Pynchon's most important characters metamorphose frequently and significantly enough to challenge the common assumption that people remain consistent. *V.* provides two examples. In his Confessions Fausto

Maijstral delineates the four very different identities he has had. He changed from "a young sovereign, dithering between Caesar and God" to a builder and family man to a nonhuman hiding in inanimateness from the horrors of war to a man of letters (pp. 286-87). Likewise, Herbert Stencil, in addition to his enduring paranoid vision, has a "repertoire of identities" (p. 51). At times, as Joseph W. Slade argues, he is a parody of Henry Adams, looking for the effects and nature of energy, which he can most easily embody as a woman (p. 51). Even some of the stereotyped characters occasionally change their identities. At one point the well-named Pig Bodine asks Rachel, " 'What do you think of Sartre's thesis that we are all impersonating an identity?' " (p. 118). His sudden intellectuality complicates him, and his question itself disputes the concept of identity. Pointsman, the cold, behavioristic scientist in *Gravity's Rainbow*, turns out also to be a poet. Pynchon creates a peculiarly inconsistent character in *Gravity's Rainbow*, Gavin Trefoil, a minor character "who can change his color from most ghastly albino up through a smooth spectrum to very deep, purplish, black" (p. 147).

Pynchon sets forth another problem about human personality by showing that at the core of many people lies a mystery. Sometimes one of his characters confronts this mystery in others. In an early story, "Low-lands," the main character leaves his mundane home for a dreamlike garbage dump and then strays even further from ordinary existence by following a gypsy girl through a maze of tunnels.[14] Later in his career Pynchon describes a more frightening possibility when he shows that a character can discover a mystery within his own personality. During his quest Slothrop begins to suspect that early in his life the rapidly growing German war machine had manipulated him. Laszlo Jamf, a German scientist whose discoveries contributed to rocket research, very likely programed Slothrop sexually, although this is not definitely established. Also, the paper company owned by Slothrop's father received a contract to print banknotes that Hjalmar Schacht used to hide the growth of German military capability. Then mystery piles on top of mystery when one of the characters claims that Jamf never existed (p. 738).

The technique of using doubles is another way in which Pynchon challenges the traditional concept of identity. At his best Pynchon uses the literary convention of the double not as Dostoevsky and others did, to make a moral point about the struggle between a person's better and worse natures, but to make a metaphysical point about the inadequacy of the prevalent notions of human personality. Some of Pynchon's doubles, however, have little importance except to add a new twist to a plot. In his first published work, "Mortality and Mercy in Vienna," two characters meet: "They faced each other like slightly flawed mirror images—different patterns of tweed, scotch bottle and pig foetus but no discrepancy in height—with Siegel experiencing a mixed feeling of discomfort and awe, and the word *Doppelgänger* had just floated into his mind."[15] A similar explicit and not very profound example is found in "Low-lands": " 'That's me, ain't it.' Not quite, it occurred to him immediately. Closer to his *Doppelgänger*, that seadog of the lusty, dark Pacific days" (p. 103). As late as *Gravity's Rainbow* Pynchon develops this motif briefly by indicating that Eventyr may "map on to Peter Sachsa" (p. 218).

Pynchon develops the double motif more originally and incisively in *V*. There Victoria—who is possibly an avatar of V. and thus possibly not a real character in the usual sense—believes in a primitive faith, including "the notion of the wraith or spiritual double, happening on rare occasions by multiplication but more often by fission, and the natural corollary which says the son is doppelgänger to the father" (p. 183). Here the double becomes more than a fictional device. Pynchon suggests that belief in it may be more rare and more justifiable than the usual conceptions of personality.

A pair of characters forming a double plays an important part in *Gravity's Rainbow*. By the time he wrote this book Pynchon had learned to dramatize and develop this motif rather than merely state it or deal with it discursively. A sailor on his way with the Russian fleet to assault the enemy during the Russo-Japanese war leaves an African woman pregnant with a child, Enzian. The child's half-brother, Tchitcherine, recognizes both the biological and the psychological implications of this relationship. One character says of him, " 'Tchitcherine is a complex man. It's almost as if . . . he thinks of Enzian as . . . another *part* of him—a black version of something inside *himself*. A something he needs to . . . liquidate' " (p. 499). His actions confirm this analysis. Pynchon casts an eerie light on this problem on the novel's next-to-last page, where he equates whiteness with death. Thus, Enzian represents life, because of his blackness, and Tchitcherine tries to liquidate him in the name of death. Pynchon also implies here the brutal treatment of blacks by whites, which he documents in the scenes in German Southwest Africa.

Pynchon's apparent insertion of himself into one of his novels is also nonrealistic. Pirate Prentice in *Gravity's Rainbow* has a Pynchonesque talent for "getting inside the fantasies of others; being able, actually, to take over the burden of *managing* them" (p. 12). Dnubietna in *V.*, however, most closely resembles Pynchon. A Maltese friend of Fausto Maijstral, he turns the horror of World War II into art, as Pynchon himself does in *Gravity's Rainbow*. Pynchon's description of Dnubietna accords with factual details of his own life and probably furnishes a clue to his artistic credo:

> Even the radical Dnubietna, whose tastes assuredly ran to apocalypse at full gallop, eventually created a world in which the truth had precedence over his engineer's politics. . . . . . The Ash Wednesday poem marked his lowest point: after that he gave up abstraction and a political rage which he later admitted was "all posturing" to be concerned increasingly with what was, not what ought to have been or what could be under the right form of government. (p. 196)

Finally, the appearance of Pynchon's characters in more than one work makes them seem less like imitations of real persons than like tools for the author. Kurt Mondaugen and Weissmann appear in both *V.* and *Gravity's Rainbow*; Clayton "Bloody" Chiclitz appears in all three novels; Pig Bodine appears in *V.*, *Gravity's Rainbow*, and "Low-lands." Pynchon treats his characters like puppets that he can take out of the box whenever he chooses rather than like imitations of actual persons.

Pynchon's settings also attack common sense and realism. For example, he stresses their symbolic dimension, often at the expense of their realistic dimension. He generally either ignores the setting's physical aspects or sketches them in quickly so that the emphasis falls on symbolic meanings. For example, the symbolic meanings of Malta's landscape play an important part in both *V.* and *Gravity's Rainbow*. This island's rockiness has dominated its geography since the rich topsoil that once covered it was stripped off centuries ago. Together with the scarcity of water, the lack of soil makes existence on Malta laborious. One can admire the resiliency that the hostile landscape has created in the Maltese, a quality that is very useful during the wars and other difficulties that dominate the action of Pynchon's books. At times this rocklike human character takes on an almost spiritual quality. In *V.* Esther asks, "What religion is it—one of the Eastern ones—where the highest condition we can attain is that of an object—a rock" (p. 93). Rocks, on the other hand, are disturbingly inanimate. Many of Pynchon's characters feel horror when metamorphosis into inanimate objects threatens them, as it often does. His creation of the hideous, near-human SHROUD, which dominates one of the most powerful scenes in *V.*, exemplifies his dramatization of this fear. A reader may legitimately ask how SHROUD differs from the Maltese. Pynchon also repeatedly shows the cruelty that results when people treat others like rocks, as many have treated the Maltese and Southwest Africans. Critics have commented on both the positive and the negative rocklike characters in Pynchon's novels, but it is best to recognize his ambivalence. In *City of Words* Tony Tanner explains this common ambivalence in contemporary American fiction by citing writers who shun both a rigidity that precludes freedom and a fluidity that precludes firmness.

The other notable feature of Malta's geography, an escarpment that divides the island in two, also has a symbolic meaning, as Pynchon's oft-cited and revealing story "Entropy" implies.[16] The narrator says of one character in it, Aubade, that "the architectonic purity of her world was constantly threatened by such hints of anarchy: gaps and excrescences and skew lines, and a shifting or tilting of planes to which she had continually to readjust lest the whole structure shiver into a disarray of discrete and meaningless signals" (p. 283). That is, she has endured the same process that creates an escarpment. This land form, then, visually represents the trauma that produced it. To humans this trauma may be personal, as it is in Aubade's case, or historical, as it is in the case of the Maltese.

The geography of another land that Pynchon uses as a setting, Southwest Africa, resembles Malta's. An escarpment divides that country, too, and symbolizes traumas of the inhabitants. Even Malta has more rainfall than the Kalahari Desert in Southwest Africa. In fact, this desert is a quintessential wasteland. As Raymond Olderman points out in *Beyond the Waste Land*, this motif recurs in contemporary American fiction, often making a comment about or evaluation of contemporary culture and its prevailing lack of morality and spirituality. Like Malta, Southwest Africa symbolizes the fate of its inhabitants. They, too, have been continual victims, contending not only with an antagonistic environment but also with invaders who inexplicably want to take that environment away from them.

Pynchon sets two of his earliest stories, "Mortality and Mercy in Vienna" and "Entropy," in Washington, D.C., another symbolic location. He names Vienna in the title of the former story not because the action takes place there but because he quotes a line from *Measure for Measure*. The party-goers in this story prefigure the decadent Whole Sick Crew of *V*. In "Mortality and Mercy" an American Indian at first stolidly and silently resists his environment, but he finally goes berserk. Similarly, Callisto, by desperately attempting to defy entropy, indirectly opposes the party-goers in *V*. In addition to the psychological dimensions of these stories, the symbolic setting, Washington, adds a low-key political dimension to them. If Dnubietna in *V*. does represent Pynchon, then these would be the early political works to which the author refers in his account of Dnubietna's poetic career.

Several critics have noted another symbolic setting that often appears in Pynchon's fiction—the underground. In *V*. the Whole Sick Crew rides the New York subways, and Pig and his Puerto Rican friends track alligators in the sewers. One can easily imagine a meaning for these underground passages, although

Pynchon has an unusual attitude toward that meaning. In *V.*
"the unconscious," Tony Tanner writes, "is comparable to a sort
of primeval sewer" (p. 166). He goes on to state correctly that in *V.*
the descent into this region turns into a "dark farce." "Low-
lands" clarifies the significance that the underground has for
Pynchon. Like the tunnels and sewers in *V.* the garbage dump
and the tunnels through which Flange follows the gypsy girl
represent the unconscious. The alluring gypsy embodies Flange's
dream of a replacement for his practical wife, who resents both
him and his friends, and the unreal setting is a suitable dream
background. This aspect of the setting thus contributes to the
important psychological themes in Pynchon's work.

Even on the rare occasions when Pynchon sketches in many
physical details of a setting he makes it symbolic, "derealizing"
physical details and thereby attacking common sense. A good
example occurs in *Gravity's Rainbow:*

> Halfway between the water and the coarse sea-grass, a long stretch
> of pipe and barbed wire rings in the wind. The black latticework is
> propped up by longer slanting braces, lances pointing out to sea. An
> abandoned and mathematical look: stripped to the force-vectors
> holding it where it is, doubled up in places one row behind another,
> moving as Pointsman and Mexico begin to move again, backward in
> thick moiré, repeated uprights in parallax against repeated
> diagonals, and the snarls of wire below interfering more at random.
> Far away, where it curves into the haze, the openwork wall goes gray.
> After last night's snowfall, each line of the black scrawl was etched in
> white. But today wind and sand have blown the dark iron bare again,
> salted, revealing, in places, brief streaks of rust . . . in others, ice and
> sunlight turn the construction to electric-white lines of energy. (p. 91)

This setting is much more than a realistic backdrop for the
action. The first sentence objectively reports a perception. In the
next sentence the scene becomes metaphoric in an unremarkable
way. There metaphors—the lattice work and the lances—
organize the perception. Then, however, scientific information
turns this scene into an elaborate and unusual metaphor. The
vectors and lines of energy have well-known meanings but the
moiré effect and parallax perhaps require explanation. As the two

characters move parallel to the fence, their perception of sections of it changes. Pynchon expresses this change metaphorically: a moiré effect is the wavelike pattern created by imposing one pattern on another; parallax is the apparent change in an object's position due to a change in an observer's position. The change becomes exponential, to use science metaphorically: the observers change the perceptual field and Pynchon changes it. Moreover, Pointsman, a Behaviorist, constantly transforms things—and people—into objects of scientific manipulation, and Mexico, a sensitive and impressive man capable of love, constantly resists this process. That is, in this scene Pynchon shows Pointsman's characteristic activity dominating Mexico's.

In addition to rendering tangible settings fantastic, Pynchon makes fantastic settings apparently tangible. Vheissu in *V.*, an exotic land that Godolphin claims to have visited, is a dream become substantial. Godolphin half-consciously recognizes its oneiric status, saying once that in Vheissu " 'dreams are not, not closer to the waking world, but somehow, I think, they do seem more real' " (pp. 155–56). About his fantasy he speaks more truthfully than he realizes. Later he takes the final step toward the truth: " 'Vheissu itself, a gaudy dream. Of what the Antarctic in this world is closest to: a dream of annihilation' " (p. 190). Godolphin describes Vheissu fully, but later even he realizes that it is only an objectification of his paranoia.

Although a full discussion of Pynchon's debts to the German film industry should be placed in the chapter on the cinema, part of that debt is apparent in his settings. Calling them Expressionistic helps to explain them; in *Gravity's Rainbow* he points out camouflage's similarity to "German Expressionist ripples" (p. 513). Possibly he borrowed some of his effects directly from German painting of the era immediately preceding World War I, particularly movements such as *Die Brücke* and *Der Blaue Reiter*. It is much more likely, however, that he borrowed ideas from the film sets that these artists influenced. The Expressionist movement, including other arts as well as painting, did not generate much interest until after the war, when some of its techniques and conceptions of art filtered into the German cinema. For example, Hermann Warm, an Expressionist painter, made the sets for the enormously influential film, *The Cabinet of Dr. Caligari* (1920). These sets and others inspired by this film feature jagged lines, sharp points, and striking contrasts between light and dark. In general, they create a scene that barely resembles ordinary objects. Pynchon's novels abound with such backdrops: characters poised against the jagged outlines of wrecked buildings, illuminated by ghostly light, or swathed in shadows. The description of the barbed wire, the gray penumbra at the points where the fence disappears into the haze, and the strange sunlight that turns the fence into "lines of energy" in the passage just quoted serves as an example.

Psychological phenomena also operate in this brief passage. As Siegfried Kracauer mentions, the Expressionists tried to make something from the war's shattered remains.[17] For instance, the original directors of *The Cabinet of Dr. Caligari* used Expressionistic means to create a strong anti-authoritarian strain, which became diluted when Wiene took over production of the film and made it, in Kracauer's words, a "translation of a madman's fantasy into pictorial terms" (p. 70). Later films, such as Fritz Lang's *Dr. Mabuse* series, followed Wiene's lead. The original *Cabinet of Dr. Caligari*, its revised version, and the films that followed its example dramatized psychological phenomena. Kracauer believes that in them "the settings amounted to a perfect transformation of material objects into emotional ornaments" (p. 69). Although capable of objectifying many emotions, Expressionism objectified most effectively the primal, negative ones such as fear and hostility. Again one can see influences on Pynchon, whose settings usually express one of these base emotions. The barbed wire, even aside from its associations with containment, produces a vague sense of uneasiness and anxiety because of the way he describes it. The Expressionists' fascination with hidden psychological mechanisms and their resultant willingness to distort make their works, like Pynchon's, anti-realistic.

As one should by now expect, Pynchon's themes differ from those of the realistic novel and from the concerns of ordinary life. Occasionally he does discuss moral or social issues, but he usually subordinates them to other issues, treats them idiosyncratically, or explores them so clearly that his meaning is obvious. As a general rule, however, he focuses on literary, epistemological, and metaphysical problems, fiercely intellectual matters of little interest to those who read novels only for recreation. Epistemological themes, including searches for information and for patterns that can create order, dominate his novels. The major metaphysical issue is the alleged existence of cabals, in particular, whether belief in them is paranoid or practical.

Finally, one needs to mention the tremendous erudition with which Pynchon develops his themes. One's arms may tire from holding up *Gravity's Rainbow* long enough to read it, but this malady is nothing compared to the aching legs a tracker of its allusions will get or to the vertigo caused by trying to fit those allusions together into a pattern. Like several contemporary writers—Jorge Luis Borges and Vladimir Nabokov come quickly to mind—Pynchon apparently has read everything. This vast knowledge distances in emotional terms a reader from Pynchon's material because it increases one's intellectual response to his work and decreases one's emotional response.

This erudition, together with several other qualities, justifies placing Pynchon's work in the category that Northrop Frye calls Menippean satire.[18] That is, it belongs in the tradition of *Gargantua and Pantagruel, Gulliver's Travels, Candide*, and other great works that appeared to be anomalous until Frye set forth their similarities. One will only distort Pynchon by insisting that he is a badly flawed realistic novelist, when he is actually a writer belonging to this other tradition. The erudition in such satires, according to Frye, permits the author, on the one hand, to satirize pedantry and, on the other, to display his own knowledge and to satirize gently his own pedantry. Incidental verse also occurs frequently in Menippean satire. In Pynchon's work the characters break into song, as if they were in a musical comedy or an opera. A loose-jointed plot and stylized rather than realistic characters are other features of these works, and Pynchon surely qualifies on both of these points. Menippean satirists, including Pynchon, try not to imitate actions but rather to depict mental attitudes, and they analyze intellectual issues rather than describe society. His pages are filled with cranks of almost every conceivable kind, as well as with a few incisive thinkers. The cranks include the psychodontist in *V.* who thinks that dental problems cause all psychological disability, but he would not appear at all strange in the third voyage of *Gulliver's Travels* among all the crazy projectors. Two mental attitudes, paranoia and anti-paranoia, recur in Pynchon's novels. The repeated emphasis on them should not surprise anyone who understands this tradition. On this point, Frye makes a point that should be a useful warning to some of Pynchon's detractors: "At its most concentrated the Menippean satire presents us with a vision of the world in terms of a single intellectual pattern. The intellectual structure built up from the story makes for violent dislocations in the customary logic of narrative, though the appearance of carelessness that results reflects only the carelessness of the reader or his tendency to judge by a novel-centered conception of fiction" (Frye, p. 310).

Edward Mendelson delineates a type of literature that he calls encyclopedic narrative, which is very similar to Frye's Menippean satire category, although Mendelson does not mention Frye.[19] Mendelson adds *Gravity's Rainbow* to other books of this type, including *The Divine Comedy, Gargantua and Pantagruel, Don Quixote, Faust, Moby-Dick* and *Ulysses.* He considers these works important not only for their intrinsic merit but also in the sense that "each major Western national culture, as it becomes fully conscious of itself as a unity, produces an encyclopedic narrative" (p. 161). In his view, *Moby-Dick* performs this function for American culture and *Gravity's Rainbow* performs it for "a new international culture, created by the technologies of instant communication and the economy of world markets" (p. 165). These narratives "attempt to render the full range of knowledge and beliefs of a national culture, while identifying the ideological perspectives from which that culture shapes and interprets its knowledge" (p. 162). According to Mendelson, among the characteristics of encyclopedic narrative are indeterminate form, exhaustive treatment of at least one science or technology, a wide range of prose styles, and a history of language.

Like all Menippean satires, Pynchon's work must be distinguished from other kinds of satire, with which it shares some characteristics. For example, Alvin P. Kernan convincingly argues that in satire "the scene is always crowded, disorderly, grotesque . . . the plot always takes the pattern of purpose followed by passion, but fails to develop beyond this point [to perception]."[20] In Pynchon's work, however, the object of satire eludes identification. In fact, he makes a major point of showing that no one can identify the enemy, who may not even exist. He clearly attacks a number of small targets, but leaves unsettled the question of whether or not they combine to form a large enemy.

Far from being pure satire, his fiction resembles tragedy in several ways. To distinguish these two modes Maynard Mack describes the latter in terms that apply fairly well to Pynchon's work:

> Where tragedy fortifies the sense of irrationality and complexity in experience because it presents us a world in which man is more victim than agent, in which our commodities prove to be our defects (and vice versa), and in which blindness and madness are likely to be symbols of insight, satire tends to fortify our feeling that life makes more immediate moral sense. In the world it offers us, madness and blindness are usually the emblems of vice and folly, evil and good are clearly distinguishable, criminals and fools are invariably responsible (therefore censurable), and standards of judgment are indubitable.[21]

Despite their complexity, their well-hidden norms, and their many victims, however, Pynchon's books differ significantly from tragedies. For one thing, he creates no tragic heroes, fully developed characters who both earn empathy from readers and obtain significant insights by suffering. Instead, he produces mainly stick-figures and then creates distance between them and his readers, and his characters, despite their sufferings, understand little more at the end of his books than they do at the beginning.

It therefore is difficult to identify Pynchon's genre. A judicious critic should probably classify his books as Menippean satire, a category whose features are only broadly defined, and not try to go beyond that, except to note that Pynchon's mixtures of traditional genres, like so many other features of his work, add to its complexity and run counter to established methods.

One can deal more easily with the comic qualities of these books, for comedy is definitely there. The humor includes slapstick—such as the adventures of a man wearing a pig suit—the grotesque, erudite in-jokes, and verbal pyrotechnics. Although different theories of comedy explain different comic passages, none will fully explain works as complex as Pynchon's. An examination of the comedy in those works will, however, help to determine which theories apply and will show how Pynchon's use of comedy reinforces his other techniques. The theory that comedy is used to establish superiority does not work at all. Although the characters' actions do make them appear inferior to the reader, as long as the existence of a plot in the novel remains possible, a reader may be troubled by the possibility of a plot in the real world and thus feel threatened, not superior to the characters. The theory of sympathy breaks down, for these books produce very little, if any, gentle laughter of concern. Even if the reader does not feel threatened, he or she may find it difficult to sympathize with such incompletely developed characters. Bergson's contention that people laugh at the mixture of the mechanical world and the vital world casts light on the comedy in Pynchon's work, but Pynchon's portrayal of the frightening implications of mechanical processes, especially their destruction of vital processes, usually precludes laughter.

In contrast, two of the major theories of comedy do apply well to Pynchon's work. The psychological theory of release explains the relation between threat and comedy that was mentioned earlier. Much of the laughter he generates is nervous. One's own reactions provide most of the evidence for this contention, and every reader will have to be his or her own judge, but many scenes that elicit laughter are certainly also frightening. The scene with SHROUD, for example, involves a reader intensely, almost convinces one of its possibility, perhaps even of its probability, but when it ends, the return to objectivity allows recognition that such events will probably not happen. Mixing concern and confidence that the object of concern will not happen releases psychological pressure and thus causes laughter.

The theory of incongruity also helps explain Pynchon's comedy. On this point one does not need evanescent data about individual responses, because the tissue of Pynchon's work consists largely of incongruities. Characters looking for evidence to support their paranoia consider the incongruities to be the intrusion of a hostile, vague force into an otherwise orderly and benign world. On the other hand, characters who accept anti-paranoia (belief that details have no relation to each other) use the same evidence to argue that nothing really controls events, otherwise there would not be such widespread incongruity. Incongruity also demonstrates the need to explain things. On this point one can usefully analyze Mickey Rooney's appearance in *Gravity's Rainbow* on a balcony during the Potsdam Conference. Such an obvious incongruity is comic. One could argue that this incident shows a plot, that only something sinister would juxtapose the conference and Mickey Rooney. In contrast, others could argue that no plot would bring together these two things and that this connection, like everything else, has to be gratuitous. More basic is the need to explain this juxtaposition, to place it in an ordering scheme.

As an examination of Pynchon's comedy shows, his work's ambiguous tone creates a critical problem. An example occurs in the crucial passage in *V.* when McClintic Sphere realizes "that the only way clear of the cool/crazy flipflop was obviously slow, frustrating and hard work. Love with your mouth shut, help without breaking your ass or publicizing it: keep cool, but care" (pp. 342–43). Critics have interpreted this passage in three ways. Raymond Olderman, considering the tone to be serious and the meaning straightforward, says that "McClintic's recognition is one of the most positive and tender moments of the book" (p. 139). At the other extreme, Tony Tanner interprets the tone by arguing that "you cannot render great emotions in a comic-strip, and 'Keep cool, but care' is just bubble talk or the sort of slogan-jargon mongered by advertisements. In proximity to the multiple parodic references which the book contains, any potentially serious emotion is bound to turn into its own caricature and join the masquerade as a costumed sentimentality" (p. 161). Irving Feldman argues that this passage fails not because it does not suit the tone of the rest of *V.* but because of a specific stylistic flaw: "Sphere's higgledy-piggledy cutely 'authentic' prose holds no charm for me."[22] If one needs to choose among these three alternatives, Tanner makes the best case. The phrasing, the context (Sphere is breaking up with his girl, Paola), and Sphere's lack of credentials as a moral preceptor make it difficult to take his pronouncement seriously. As to Feldman, more than mere stylistic infelicity militates against the seriousness of that passage. In the final analysis, however, one would do better not to choose definitively. Pynchon in this passage and many others creates an ambiguous tone that reduces certainty. Although it would be comforting to believe that all one need do is keep cool but care, Pynchon does not allow such a clear solution.

Despite the ambiguity, the tone is almost always detached. The "nose job" section of *V.* is disturbing, perhaps offensive, yet even there Pynchon creates a nearly clinical effect. Similarly, in *Gravity's Rainbow* he distances the horrors of World War II. Sometimes this distancing turns into an ironic, macabre joke, such as the one about the German atrocities in Southwest Africa falling far short of those in the extermination camps but still being "pretty good." In instances like the last one Pynchon sacrifices a good deal to maintain the detached tone that accommodates the highly intellectual content of his books.

As he does with the other elements of fiction, Pynchon uses point of view partly to create confusion and thus to cast doubt on conventional ways of making sense of things both in novels and in the real world. One cause of the confusion is the appearance of old-fashioned, even frequently discredited methods in books that are in many ways very avant-garde. As Edward Mendelson points out, "Pynchon uses omniscient narrators, direct addresses to the audience, characters capable of heightened speech (in the form of a song), authorial judgments on character and situation, verse epigraphs—all the paraphernalia of the loose baggy monsters of an earlier age of fiction."[23] Such intentional confusion may also be caused, however, by sophisticated handling of point of view, quite apart from mixtures of old and new techniques. In fact, Pynchon's handling of point of view has become more sophisticated as his career has progressed. In *V.* he tries in various ways to cast doubt on the sources of the information that is presented. In one section already cited, he prefaces an episode with the admonition, "The rest was impersonation and dream" (p. 52). At another point the narrator suddenly asks "Was it the Dance of Death brought up to date?" (p. 282). No one answers this question, so the incident's status remains in doubt. More subtly, later he arranges the plot so that a juxtaposition will make an incident doubtful. After Fausto learns of his wife's death, he experiences a "blank space" and then immediately has his important encounter with the bad priest, who may be an avatar of V. (p. 320). His blacking out, an event not mentioned by critics who discuss the succeeding passage, casts doubt on the credibility of the account that follows.

Similarly, much of the narrative of *V.* filters through Herbert Stencil's consciousness. For example, he tells Eigenvalue part of the story of Kurt Mondaugen. The otherwise silent listener interrupts once to raise suspicions, " 'I only think it strange that he should remember an unremarkable conversation, let alone in that much detail, thirty-four years later' " (p. 231). Immediately before Stencil's narrative begins, Pynchon justifies Eigenvalue's skepticism. Stencil had heard the story directly from Mondaugen, "yet the next Wednesday afternoon at Eigenvalue's office, when Stencil retold it, the yarn had undergone considerable change: had become, as Eigenvalue put it, Stencilized" (p. 211). This Stencilization can easily slip past unnoticed. Stencil, like Henry Adams—whose influence, sometimes explicitly acknowledged, pervades *V.*, *Gravity's Rainbow*, and "Entropy"—refers to himself in the third person. This device creates an illusion of detached observation, but the author frequently indicates that it is merely an illusion. In fact, he suggests frequently that Stencil's obsession with V. amounts to a paranoid vision that distorts all his perceptions.

Other passages in *V.*, such as the Confessions of Fausto Maijstral, further complicate the novel's point of view. In that section Fausto writes about himself, shifting back and forth between first-person and third-person narration. There, too, the principal narrator of *V.* is silent. Chapter three, as Richard Patteson shows, has a particularly enigmatic point of view.[24] He goes on to clarify the points of view in other sections of *V.* Changes in point of view and the undercutting of narrators make it difficult for a reader to determine what to believe. Pynchon's meaning, though an old one, needs to be stated frequently: point of view matters. He shows that in a novel information does not come to readers directly from an author by means of an objective, virtually nonexistent reporter. Rather, someone discovers and shapes it.

In his next novel, *The Crying of Lot 49*, Pynchon's results are the same but his means are more carefully interrelated and more clever. He tells the story in the third person, making comments that establish the narrator as, if not omniscient, at least privileged to much information, including the contents of Oedipa's mind. The narrator frequently makes comments like "out at the airport Oedipa, feeling invisible, eavesdropped on a poker game" (p. 90). In other words, Pynchon creates a center of consciousness. Oedipa remains at the action's center, yet she does not tell her own story. On the one hand, by the third-person arrangement the author gains the distancing necessary to raise philosophical issues. On the other hand, as would a writer using first-person narration, he dramatizes a mind grappling to make sense of its surroundings, which is his major concern. He uses this method of narration to delineate only the surface of his center of consciousness. A deeper probing would require either too much confusion produced by Oedipa's chaotic musings or her solution of the epistemological puzzles that baffle her, which would make them both less interesting and oversimplified.

In *Gravity's Rainbow* Pynchon combines the strengths of the points of view of his two previous novels. He again uses the center-of-consciousness method of *The Crying of Lot 49*, with the same results. However, he creates multiple centers of consciousness: Slothrop, Pökler, and others alternate as the filter for the action. The voice that reports on the centers of consciousness thus is more complicated than the voice of *The Crying of Lot 49*. The mixture of these centers makes it difficult to determine what the voice itself thinks about almost anything. This does not mean that because of its inability to find the truth it merely presents a variety of possibilities without choosing among them. Although the voice does not judge, it cogently organizes information from the characters' own insufficient organizations.

For the most part, Pynchon's images and symbols make more sense in the context of the nonliterary disciplines to be discussed later, but a quick examination here of some of their similarities will show that these elements of fiction work consistently with the other elements. Some images recur, such as the tunnels and other underground places in several works, the bananas in *Gravity's Rainbow*, and the kazoos in several works. This recurrence, together with the strangeness of the images, makes them seem to be important. Sometimes an image is described so vividly that it seems significant; for example, "as for Melanie, her lover had provided her with mirrors, dozens of them. Mirrors with handles, with ornate frames, full-length and pocket mirrors came to adorn the loft wherever one turned to look" (*V.*, p. 383).

In addition to hinting at the significance of these images, the author insures that they do not exactly take on meanings but become associated with certain contexts. One can easily place the tunnels, as I have mentioned, in a psychological context by equating them with the unconscious, although to do this leaves the image somewhat imprecise and certainly does not exhaust the image's meaning. The bananas, because of the lusty characters who appear with them, have phallic overtones. Pynchon himself provides ingenious contexts for the kazoos. Very late in *Gravity's Rainbow* he writes:

> Säure has had ex-Peenemünde engineers, propulsion-group people, working on a long-term study of optimum hashpipe design, and guess what—in terms of flow rate, heat-transfer, control of air-to-smoke ratio, the perfect shape turns out to be that of the classical *kazoo!*
>
> Yeah, another odd thing about the kazoo: the knuckle-thread above the reed there is exactly the same as a thread in a light-bulb socket. (p. 745)

Therefore his images reveal their importance and easily fit into a context, or into several different contexts, but they rarely become completely clear. On this matter Richard Poirier says, "The persistent paranoia of all the important characters [in *Gravity's Rainbow*] invests any chance detail with the power of an omen."[25] That is, the images' special properties place a reader in the same difficulty that bothers the characters: they must interpret details and form them into meaningful patterns. John P. Leland makes a similar point about the total effect of *The Crying of Lot 49*.[26] He perceptively comments that the reader, like Oedipa, must find ways to deal with the information that inundates him or her.

Although many of his images do not have enough clear meaning to qualify as symbols, Pynchon does create a few symbols, such as the central ones of each novel: V., the Tristero, and the rocket. V. represents a destructive force, although its nature remains a puzzle. R. W. B. Lewis's contention that "she is Satan himself in the guise of the Whore of Babylon," like other very specific interpretations, restricts the meaning too much.[27] The Tristero's meaning expands from an alternative postal system to a society that is an alternative to contemporary America. The rocket represents human self-destructiveness, apocalypse, and the dangers of technology. Alan J. Friedman and Manfred Puetz incisively state why the rocket is such a powerful and multifaceted symbol: "Both life and the rocket rise from the rubble, burn bright for a while, and then return to the rubble to be rewoven into life again."[28] That is, both the rocket and life oppose entropy. All these meanings persist despite the questions about whether the three things really exist. Like V., however, the other two symbols resist specific, limited interpretations. In addition to generally agreed upon meanings, all three have unspecifiable meanings.

The final element of fiction, style, is crucial to Pynchon's work. Throughout his career he has mentioned the difficulty of fitting language to reality, of creating an effective prose style. A character in "Entropy" agonizes: " 'Tell a girl: "I love you." No trouble with two-thirds of that, it's a closed circuit. Just you and she. But that nasty four-letter word in the middle, *that's* the one you have to look out for. Ambiguity. Redundance. Irrelevance, even' " (p. 285). In a surrealistic passage in *Gravity's Rainbow* he includes this description:

> At the end of the mighty day in which he gave us in fiery letters across the sky all the words we'd ever need, words we today enjoy, and fill our dictionaries with, the meek voice of little Tyrone Slothrop, celebrated

ever after in tradition and song, ventures to filter upward to the Kid's attention: "You never did '*the*,' Kenosha Kid!"

These changes on the text "You never did the Kenosha Kid" are occupying Slothrop's awareness. (p. 61)

Here overzealous playing with language makes it almost meaningless. At other times, in spite of a character's best attempt, language can convey only a little meaning.

The two most important of Pynchon's stylistic effects— transformation and foregrounding—deserve careful scrutiny. By transformation is meant making it appear that the author, through his style, is mediating experience. An analysis of a passage from *Gravity's Rainbow* supports this contention. The openings of novels have often served as the subject of such analyses:

A screaming comes across the sky. It had happened before, but there is nothing to compare it to now.

It is too late. The Evacuation still proceeds, but it's all theatre. There are no lights inside the cars. No light anywhere. Above him lift girders old as an iron queen, and glass somewhere far above that would let the light of day through. But it's night. He's afraid of the way the glass will fall—soon—it will be a spectacle: the fall of a crystal palace. But coming down in total blackout, without one glint of light, only great invisible crashing.

Inside the carriage, which is built on several levels, he sits in velveteen darkness, with nothing to smoke, feeling metal nearer and farther rub and connect, steam escaping in puffs, a vibration in the carriage's frame, a poising, an uneasiness, all the others pressed in around, feeble ones, second sheep, all out of luck and time: drunks, old veterans still in shock from ordnance 20 years obsolete, hustlers in city clothes, derelicts, exhausted women with more children than it seems could belong to anyone, stacked about among the rest of the things to be carried out to salvation. Only the nearer faces are visible at all, and at that only as half-silvered images in a view finder, green-stained VIP faces remembered behind bulletproof windows speeding through the city. . . .

They have begun to move. They pass in line, out of the main station, out of downtown, and begin pushing into older and more desolate parts of the city. Is this the way out? Faces turn to the windows, but no one dares ask, not out loud. Rain comes down. No, this is not a disentanglement from, but a progressive *knotting into*— they go in under archways, secret entrances of rotted concrete that only looked like loops of an underpass . . . certain trestles of blackened wood have moved slowly by overhead, and the smells begun of coal from days far to the past, smells of naphtha winters, of Sundays when no traffic came through, of the coral-like and mysteriously vital growth, around the blind curves and out the lonely spurs, a sour smell of rolling-stock absence, of maturing rust, developing through those emptying days brilliant and deep, especially at dawn, with blue shadows to seal its passage, to try to bring events to Absolute Zero . . . and it is poorer the deeper they go . . . ruinous secret cities of poor, places whose *names he has never heard* . . . the walls break down, the roofs get fewer and so do the chances for light. The road, which ought to be opening out into a broader highway, instead has been getting narrower, more broken, cornering tighter and tighter until all at once, much too soon, they are under the final arch: brakes grab and spring terribly. It is a judgment from which there is no appeal. (pp. 3–4)

A cursory examination reveals that the hypothesis about transformation deserves more meticulous testing. Even the diction metamorphoses, for the passage has many participles and other verbals, words changed from verbs into other parts of speech. Using images and figures of speech constructed from perceptions, Pynchon begins to make this setting and action comprehensible. Like the scene cited earlier in which he describes a length of barbed wire, this scene contains imagery that resembles the sets of Expressionistic German films: the light and dark, especially in the second paragraph, and the jagged lines (the girders, the falling crystal palace, the connecting metal, the archways, the rotten concrete, the broken road and the final arch). The allusion to Rilke's *Sonnets to Orpheus* in the first sentence and the reference to Absolute Zero are literary and scientific allusions. A reference to religion lurks in the background: the light images, the references to salvation, and especially the "final arch" and "judgment" at the end of this passage have overtones of apocalypse, a suitable analogy in this scene about the London Blitz. Unusual ordering principles in these paragraphs also make it seem that a mind is transforming the discrete details into a pattern. The play of light and shadow helps to unify the second paragraph; the perceptions of the unnamed observer hold the third paragraph together; the movement of people past the scenes in the fourth paragraph unifies it.

The hypothesis can be rephrased: in Pynchon's novels his style implies that he is turning experience into comprehensible terms. Pynchon imitates neither Hemingway, who tries to come as close as possible to presenting experience itself, nor Faulkner and James, who present experience after it has been shaped. In other words, Pynchon concentrates on the process of organizing data, not on unorganized data or the result of such organizing.

Critics have noticed the second important characteristic of Pynchon's prose, its foregrounding, in other writers. Tony Tanner uses this term to describe the style of some other writers and attributes it to the Prague school of linguists.[29] A foregrounded style focuses attention not on the words' referents but on the writer's verbal performance. Writing about an example in *Moby Dick* that could be called foregrounding, Richard Poirier claims, "The agitations of voice, the playfulness through which symbols emerge and then dissolve, the mixture of incantatory, Biblical, polite, and vernacular language in this and other American books—these are what demand our attention altogether more than do ideas or themes extracted by critics in the interest of tidying up what is mysterious or confused."[30] Such a style continually reminds a reader that an author has made the work and rules over it as the dominant sensibility, surpassing the characters in importance. Leo Spitzer, writing about some of Cervantes' linguistic quirks, makes the same point, calling the effect perspectivism when it helps create so many viewpoints that each one deflects the reader back to the author. In *Don Quixote*, he contends, "Things are represented, not for what they are in themselves, but only as things spoken about or thought about."[31] To put it another way, foregrounding helps create a work dominated by the author's constant creation of order. The most spectacular example of Pynchon's foregrounding occurs in *The Crying of Lot 49* when some characters perform a pseudo-Jacobean revenge tragedy. In addition to a plot summary,

Pynchon provides a few lines, a stylistic tour de force that reads like a parody until one remembers the inflated rhetoric of that subgenre; then it reads like an imitation. One passage is:

> The swan has yielded but one hollow quill,
> The hapless mutton, but his tegument;
> Yet what, transmuted, swart and silken flows
> Between, was neither plucked not harshly flayed,
> But gathered up, from wildly different beasts. (p. 49)

The concept of foregrounding will be useful only if one can specify its causes. Foregrounding depends on a reader's surprise; therefore, certain qualities that appear more often than usual in prose of the type being considered produce foregrounding. Also, many of these qualities must be present, because the cumulative effect of only a few will not cause enough surprise. Pynchon's prose does contain many of those qualities, even though a few qualities that can cause foregrounding rarely appear, as another look at the first four paragraphs of *Gravity's Rainbow* shows. One, repetition, occurs mainly in the light and dark images, but Pynchon generally varies his diction and sentence structure. He includes no foreign words in this passage, although he uses this method often throughout the novel as a whole, incorporating names and terms from a dizzying variety of languages. He rarely creates attention-getting rhythmic qualities.

One of the distinguishing marks of foregrounded prose, variety, appears frequently in his work. In this passage, the levels of diction vary widely from the colloquial to the academically formal. Sentence length varies from 3 to 149 words, the longest and shortest sentences being next to each other. In prose the frequency of phrases more suitable to poetry because of their compactness and lambency also produces this effect. In addition to his frequent and effective metaphors, Pynchon's imaginative adjectives, such as "emptying days brilliant and deep," belong to this category. Another possible cause of foregrounding, oddity, plays a large role. The syntax and, even more, the jamming together in one sentence of two or more normal sentences are examples. An unusually wide range of punctuation is used. Often ellipses or dashes tenuously hold together the wandering sentences. Elsewhere in his work the recurrence of strange words such as "wha," "wiv," "a-and" and "Nueva York," although annoying, constitutes another oddity. Between two possible causes of foregrounding, overemphasis and underemphasis, Pynchon chooses the former, as his many comparative and superlative forms show. The frenzied pace also creates fore-grounding; as Richard Poirier notes: "In the style and its rapid transitions he tries to match the dizzying tempos, the accelerated shifts from one mode of experience to another [of] contemporary media and movement" ("Rocket Power," p. 60). Finally, his arcane diction calls attention to itself. Examples are "second sheep" and "iron queen," which appear to be inventions, although the latter may be a variation on a medieval torture device, the iron maiden.

Lawrence C. Wolfley makes a perceptive comment about Pynchon's prose style and thereby identifies an important effect of its foregrounding, as well as of some of its other characteristics. Wolfley points out that *Gravity's Rainbow* is full of death, which is clear, and he continues that this novel's content "affirms death," which is not clear at all. His useful comment about style follows: "The style affirms life, since the intuitive basis of that marvelously poetic and spontaneous prose is the author's own enactment of what [Norman O.] Brown calls 'an erotic sense of reality.' "[32] Wolfley concludes his article by developing this point: "Nothing really matters but individual freedom, and Pynchon knows that the best defense of freedom is not Heisen-berg's principle of indeterminancy or even dialectics, but the miracle of language itself—language, an irreducibly intuitive symbolic process."

Thus, in Pynchon's work all the elements of fiction work together to dispute commonsense ways of understanding things. Pynchon, however, *does not* imply that the world is absurd. This point needs great emphasis, lest the unfortunate strain of absurdist criticism continue to claim Pynchon as a subject and thereby to distort his meaning. Book reviewers, presumably influenced by Camus, have made remarks like the following about *V.*: "Pynchon, half mocking, half serious, has no intention of allowing the meaning of his book to crystallize."[33] This critic, forgetting both the difficulty of proving a negative and the intentional fallacy and not admitting that his failure to find a meaning may be his own fault, offers no evidence for his claim. Another critic offers a more sophisticated version of the same point, claiming that in *V.* there is a "tension, not only within the characters but also between the characters who are reluctantly learning meanings by making connections and the narrator who, for the reader, is calling these meanings into question, not by denial but by comic multiplication of connections."[34] Like the previous writer, this one sees only the cancellation of some meanings and assumes that this suffices to make Pynchon "absurd." In the same vein, another critic charges that Pynchon "means to inventory and then jettison all the meanings of the past before launching our civilization into the great nothingness."[35] Pynchon has probably omitted a few "meanings of the past" and, although poets may be the unacknowledged legislators of the world, they cannot "launch our civilization into the great nothingness," whatever that is.

The perplexing question about the presence of meaning in Pynchon's work becomes easier if one differentiates between Pynchon and his characters. The characters certainly have difficulty in finding meaning. The plots of the three novels move forward largely because a main character in each searches for meaning. In *Gravity's Rainbow* the Zone, the no-man's land between the contending forces at the end of the war, gradually begins to represent for some characters the condition of inevitable meaninglessness. Poignantly describing it, Pynchon writes, "Down here are only wrappings left in the light, in the dark: images of the Uncertainty" (p. 303). Like others, the exploited Hereros search the Zone for the key that will give them meaning. These searches, however, do not demonstrate that Pynchon cannot find meaning.

Specific examples will show the distinction between Pynchon's meaning and that for which the characters search. Consider three discrete bits of information from *Gravity's Rainbow*: Herero villages are circular, the benzene ring is circular, the mandala is circular. Circularity, a matter of perception, becomes meaningful when placed in a context. The shape of the Herero villages can simply be called a historical fact. The benzene ring became comprehensible when Kekulé recognized its circularity. Jung and others have explained in psychological terms the mandala's circularity by claiming that it represents a fully developed personality. Thus, three nonliterary disciplines make meaningful something that had before been merely intelligible. Next, one can try to subsume all three facts within one discipline by arguing that their yearning for the fullness represented by the Mandala caused the Hereros to build circular villages and caused Kekulé to envision the benzene ring's shape. Unfortunately, these cause-and-effect relations probably cannot be proved. Also unfortunately, the multiplicity of valid disciplines needed to clarify many individual puzzles causes intolerable confusion.

The characters often find the world intelligible and understand parts of it, but then they try to explain pieces of data by referring to inappropriate disciplines, or they recognize that more than one discipline works and they panic because they cannot choose among them. Pynchon, however, takes another step. He clarifies the operation of the three disciplines, showing how they explain things. The villages, the benzene ring, and the mandalas become part of his circle imagery, which helps to unify the novel and enriches its meaning by relating previously separate phenomena to each other. For example, the circle images reinforce his theme of eternal return, a view of human existence and of time that he contrasts to linear conceptions of time and restrictive conceptions of human potential. At the same time, by tying together these circle images Pynchon reveals himself, the presiding force in the book, at work. His pattern making differs in scope and effectiveness from the pattern making of his characters, paranoid as well as nonparanoid.

A cursory look, then, suggests that Pynchon creates Surrealistic art, a type distinguished, according to Arnold Hauser, by "the meticulous naturalism of the details and the arbitrary combination of their relationships."[36] This apparent arbitrariness has provoked the cries of absurdity from critics. Far from being arbitrary, however, he carefully relates details to each other. To have a better chance to recognize these relations one must consider another of Hauser's points: "All art is a game with and a fight against chaos: it is always advancing more and more dangerously towards chaos and rescuing more and more extensive provinces of the spirit from its clutch" (p. 246). To put it another way, art, by creating form where none existed, inevitably creates meaning. Looking chaos in the eye, Pynchon has not capitulated by labeling the world chaotic; rather, he has provided a more expansive conception of human potential for those able to understand his accomplishment.

Although Pynchon's characters often misunderstand or do not know the reasons for their need of ways to organize information, they realize that they do need some organizing principles. This need becomes clear to the characters in Pynchon's first book and is more explicit in later works. His story "The Secret Integration," for example, which was published the year after *V.*, describes some small boys' methods of making sense of the world. Finding the reality of the adult world repulsive, they first invent an elaborate scheme for taking over their community. Then, alarmed and confused by their town's racial attitudes, they invent an imaginary Black playmate: a very impressive fiction, not a mere boyish prank. They thus add meaning to their lives and assume a moral position superior to that of the adults. In *V.* Herbert Stencil claims that without means of organizing data humans face alone a horrible void. Meditating on man's inhumanity to man, he thinks, "Ten million dead. Gas. Passchendaele. Let that be now a large figure, now a chemical formula, now an historical account. But dear Lord, not the Nameless Horror" (p. 431). At this point one needs to be sure of Pynchon's meaning. The Nameless Horror, if it exists objectively and not merely among Stencil's paranoid symptoms, lies at the place where Pynchon begins, not at the place where he ends. That is, the horror, if it exists, quickly dissipates when it becomes comprehensible. Critics who stress Pynchon's fear of, or fascination with, a void wrench into reverse the human mind's natural tendency to organize data, which Pynchon describes. For example, in *Gravity's Rainbow* psychologists who administer Rorschach tests assume that the person taking the test will try to structure the blot. This primitive organizing happens not out of fear but because it is an almost inevitable human mental operation.

Occasionally, heretical characters in the novels think that they can easily understand their experiences. Most commonly they cite as an authority Wittgenstein's "the world is everything that is the case." In *V.* Weissmann quotes it in 1922, the year during which the first English edition of the *Tractatus* appeared. Wittgenstein's cryptic comment probably means that things simply exist, unmediated by anything else and directly comprehensible. (Later he changed his mind and became pessimistic about human attempts to describe reality.) Pynchon shows in two ways that Weissmann errs. First, Weissmann receives radio signals that he considers to be in code. After he removes every third letter, "GODMEANTNUURK" remains. He treats this as an anagram and finds hidden in it "Kurt Mondaugen," one of his companions in Southwest Africa. However, if one makes some spaces in the sequences of letters and allows for eccentric spelling, one gets "God meant New York." In other words, Pynchon has arranged the code to show that Weissmann's interpretation of it goes astray because it is too ingenious. Second, Weissmann in *Gravity's Rainbow* becomes Blicero, an avatar of death, who treats other humans as things that simply are the case and may be killed, transformed into things that are not the case. In other words, Pynchon suggests that believing the world to be easily comprehensible can narcotize one's moral concern.

The dangers of incorrectly organizing information do not make it any less important for people to try to organize it correctly. Raymond Olderman points out one such danger: "There is no mysterious force behind V., but there is our misplaced impulse to uncover some Power external to man which is the source of our dream of annihilation—the spiritual yearning of wastelanders who live without mythology and feel compelled to construct one from the outrageous but stony materials of modern fact" (p. 137). Olderman seems to imply that one does better to leave the "stony facts" unconnected, but this will not do because incomprehension has no merit.

Although one had better not choose to take experience and information as they come, one certainly can choose from among possible ways to organize them. Pynchon dramatizes these choices partly by shaping his narrative so as to incorporate them and partly by having his characters choose. For example, sometimes the narrator uses metaphors based on methods of organizing data. Of Pynchon's oeuvre so far, Poirier helpfully writes, "All three books take enormous, burdensome responsibilities for the forces at work in the world around them, for those 'assemblies' of life, like movies, comics, and behavioristic psychology, that go on outside the novel and make of reality a fiction even before a novelist can get to it" ("Rocket Power," p. 62). Unfortunately, Poirier has little space in his review to develop this insight. James Dean Young most fully discusses Pynchon's use of nonliterary disciplines. Like several other critics, he claims that Pynchon stops after nullifying the nonliterary disciplines that he uses, but Young does cogently discuss the role of history and geography in Pynchon's first two novels. The latter discipline proves to be slippery, continually wiggling over into setting, history, and other things. Young devotes only four pages to these disciplines, but he has started off in the right direction.

No critic has discussed at a length of even four pages Pynchon's literary fictions: his own methods of organizing information and of evaluating nonliterary methods. Until now scattered comments have constituted the whole of this line of analysis. In addition to the comments I have cited, W. T. Lhamon, Jr., has made an incisive observation: "Our best fictions will always be about the need for more adequate fictions, about the construction of life's meaning from scratch" (p. 28). No one has made a better brief remark about the most fruitful approach to Pynchon's work. Similarly, John P. Leland notices that "*The Crying of Lot 49* is a fiction which explores the possibilities of language and fiction themselves" (p. 46). Leland explains that "Pynchon's art stands as a profound denial of the mimetic, and criticism which insists on a mimetic function can only offer us a superficial understanding" (p. 47). After an illuminating comparison to the work of Borges, he continues that while reading *The Crying of Lot 49* "we begin to question not only the fictional nature of fiction but the fictional quality of 'reality' as well." It is this direction—the analysis of Pynchon's oblique comments on the creation of fictions by nonliterary disciplines and by literature, which a few critics have tentatively broached—that this study will take.

2.

Science and Technology

The scientific and technological information in Pynchon's books is responsible, to a large extent, for their obscurity. One can deal efficiently with it by proceeding in two stages. First, one can see how Pynchon uses individual bits of data. To do so, one of course must know what each of the bits means. Second, one can see how Pynchon adopts for his own purposes scientific means of organizing data. For example, he frequently refers to the Second Law of Thermodynamics, often called the principle of entropy. Scientific laws synthesize because, as Stephen Toulmin shows, they "express the form of a regularity rather than merely expressing a piece of data or even a regularity."[1] Pynchon also contrasts a cause-and-effect epistemology with a statistical epistemology. He refers often to cybernetics and mathematics, two synthesizing disciplines. The avowed purpose of cybernetics is to synthesize parts of other scientific disciplines. About the synthesizing capacity of mathematics Toulmin writes, "Complex sets of exact inferring-techniques as we have need of in physics can be, and tend to be, cast in a mathematical form" (p. 33).

Pynchon adapts to literary purposes both raw information and these means for synthesizing, using them to construct metaphors, develop characters and plots, and otherwise reconstitute in his distinctive way the elements of fiction that seem so chaotic when analyzed in the usual way. These unusual literary purposes and the unfamiliar scientific information in his work do cause obscurity, but despite this obscurity, Pynchon's use of information enriches his books.

Pynchon refers most often to scientific information that was discovered or became important during World War II and the information that resulted from that period's scientific developments. In fact, he implies that these developments may have influenced the course of history more than have the political and social changes that the war caused. Many others agree with his assessment. Arthur Porter, for example, claims that "all in all the impact of World War II military technology on the world of today has been extraordinary."[2] Porter considers servomechanisms and computers to be examples of important technology developed during that era. In *Gravity's Rainbow* Pynchon implies this same point about the scientific advances of that time as he delineates the war's scientific background, especially developments that have played an important role in postwar history. In contrast, although the political events of the war years are well known, Pynchon rarely emphasizes them. For example, his characters—scientists and nonscientists alike—react more often to scientific information than to political events. At the extreme, one of the characters considers the possibility that the war is no more than a huge scientific laboratory and that politicians and military leaders set policy so as to maximize scientific and technological progress.   To elucidate this information one must begin with the rocket, the primary symbol and focal point of *Gravity's Rainbow*. In fact, nearly all the important scientific and technological information in Pynchon's novels and short stories focuses on either rocketry or fields that were advanced by efforts to improve rockets or to defend against them. Pynchon even sees sexual implications in the rocket; it is not accidental that in *Gravity's Rainbow* Slothrop's sexual relationships correlate with rocket landings. One character understands the rocket's sexuality thus: "Katje has understood the great airless arc as a clear allusion to certain secret lusts that drive the planet and herself . . . toward a terminal orgasm" (p. 223). Throughout this novel Pynchon also develops the motif of the rocket's masculinity. Enzian, a Herero who joins the search for rocket 00000, learns that "the Rocket was an entire system *won*, away from the feminine darkness, held against the entropies of lovable but scatterbrained Mother Nature: that was the first thing he was obliged by Weissmann to learn, his first step toward citizenship in the Zone" (p. 324). Pynchon hints that Weissmann, the German rocket chief, has a homosexual attachment to Enzian and to the young boy who rides inside the rocket near the novel's end. Sexuality also paradoxically opposes the rocket and its meanings, for some of the people who work on it or search for it save themselves through sexual love from its total dominance.

The rocket also has implications for the philosophy of history that show another way to arrange information about it into a pattern. Nora Dodson-Truck begins to believe that she is gravity: *"I am Gravity. I am That against which the Rocket must struggle, to which the prehistoric wastes submit and are transmuted to the very substance of History"* (p. 639). In this view, history records battles against waste: inanimateness and other anti-human qualities. To extend this metaphor's implications, history is formed as each age rises above its predecessor. Nora, however, fails to mention the other half of a rocket's flight, the downward movement from the point where gravity begins to have more force than the effect of the initial impetus. If history is a rocket, it has a parabolic course, rising but then falling to a Spenglerian collapse or to an apocalypse. The war and the psychological and social conditions in *Gravity's Rainbow* support this belief that the world will soon collapse, and the novel ends as a rocket is about to destroy a movie theater in which the readers appear to be sitting.

During World War II, rocket programs hastened the development of plastics, as scientists synthesized new plastics or improved old ones to make parts for rockets and after the war used these plastics for nonmilitary purposes and applied the knowledge that they had gained in developing plastics to solve other problems.[3] For example, scientists developed PMMA for cockpit covers, polyethylene for radar, and PTFE for atomic fission. Plastic as a material has also interested novelists because certain of its qualities have made it seem representative of our times. The simple, repeated chemical units that form the molecules make plastics a fitting analogy for a social structure composed of many simple, nearly identical persons. The molecules of one of the two types of plastics, the thermoplastics, are not chemically joined. One can draw analogies here with loose social bonds. The extreme moldability of plastics has been a major source of their usefulness, and again a social analogy is suggested. All of these phenomena, as well as plastic-like artificiality, are prominent in the society that Pynchon describes. His characters, often almost indistinguishable one from another, wander around forming unstable bonds with each other and falling victim to stronger forces that mold them at will.

By imagining the plastic Imipolex G Pynchon also adds his own meanings to this material. Jamf, the evil scientist who may have programmed Slothrop, invented Imipolex G, so it, too, is probably evil. Its development also shows the influence of international corporate cartels, since Jamf at the time of his discovery worked for IG Farben, and Shell later partially controlled the patent. To some people the history of Imipolex G therefore looks like a commercial plot. Plastics are aromatic chemicals, so Kekulé's dream of the benzene ring and all the associations that Pynchon draws from it attach themselves like carbon molecules to the motif of plastics. In this case, too, science has renounced its neutrality; the plastic synthesized for the rocket will serve the German war effort. Pynchon makes this military use appear inevitable by alluding to "Plasticity's virtuous triad of Strength, Stability and Whiteness (*Kraft, Standfestigkeit, Weisse*: how often these were taken for Nazi graffiti)" (p. 250). These first two qualities apply to stable plastics: the thermosets, which have strong molecular bonds. This statement almost makes plastic seem like a distinctively Nazi substance by comparing its physical properties to that society's ideals. Thus, going well beyond making obvious metaphors, he adds symbolic meanings to his work.

He also sees sexual meanings in plastic. For example, some of the orgiastic characters in *Gravity's Rainbow* dress a girl in Imipolex G. She admits afterward, "Nothing I ever wore, before or since, aroused me quite as much as Imipolex" (p. 488). More than two hundred pages later Pynchon explains why it excites her: "Imipolex G is the first plastic that is actually *erectile*. Under suitable stimuli, the chains grow cross-links, which stiffen the molecule and increase intermolecular attraction so that this Peculiar Polymer runs far outside the known phase diagrams, from limp rubbery amorphous to amazing perfect tesselation, hardness, brilliant transparency" (p. 699). In other words, if the girl dressed in plastic stimulated it sufficiently the plastic erected and they had a bizarre kind of intercourse. As an objective account of reality this statement does not convince, but as a comment on the sexuality of Pynchon's characters it does. Sex with a piece of plastic could not differ very much from the kind of virtually inanimate sex practiced by characters such as The Whole Sick Crew in *V*.

Plastic relates to one of the most important themes of *Gravity's Rainbow*. In a statement during a séance Walter Rathenau identifies this theme as well as another, which is developed mainly in conjunction with descriptions of the rocket: " 'You must ask two questions. First, what is the real nature of synthesis? And then: what is the real nature of control?' " (p. 167). Rathenau, "prophet and architect of the cartelized state," coordinator of the German economy during the war, and "a philosopher with a vision of the postwar State," is well qualified to identify the processes that currently shape human existence (pp. 164–65). The synthesis that resulted in the creation of plastics is disturbing as well as promising because of "Plasticity's central canon: that chemists were no longer to be at the mercy of Nature" (p. 249). Nature, no longer inviolate and self-enclosed, has capitulated to the scientists and has become a source of weapons and of goods that will allow companies to extend their dominion. Gravity itself is an ally of the synthesizers, since it hugs "to its holy center the wastes of dead species, gathered, packed, transmuted, realigned, and rewoven molecules to be taken up again by the coal-tar Kabbalists of the other side . . . still finding new molecular pieces, combining and recombining them into new synthetics" (p. 590). Moreover, coal, which furnishes many of the building blocks for the synthesizers, is "the very substance of death . . . earth's excrement" (p. 166). Synthesis, therefore, is not simply a boon to humanity.

Pynchon has some interest in another startling scientific development that occurred during World War II. In *The Human Use of Human Beings* Norbert Wiener says that during the Battle of Britain "the problem of anti-aircraft fire control made a new generation of engineers familiar with the notion of a communication addressed to a machine."[4] Successful communication with a missile makes even more disappointing the noise-plagued human conversation of Pynchon's characters. Their conversation also makes communication with things seem natural and even makes almost credible the conversation with SHROUD, the most vivid of Pynchon's allusions to this "advance." Thus, the theme of communication, which has been important throughout Pynchon's literary career and is dominant in *The Crying of Lot 49*, is connected to the scientific themes of *Gravity's Rainbow*, because much of the plot involves the efforts of the British to defend against German rockets.

Pynchon once creates a metaphor out of information from electronics, a field that grew tremendously as scientific workers learned to control the rockets. In *Gravity's Rainbow* Kurt Mondaugen forms an inventive metaphor about a triode (a vacuum tube composed of plate, cathode, and grid):

> In his electro-mysticism, the triode was as basic as the cross in Christianity. Think of the ego, the self that suffers a personal history bound to time, as the grid. The deeper and true Self is the flow between cathode and plate. The constant, pure flow. Signals—sense-data, feelings, memories relocating—are put onto the grid, and modulate the flow. We live lives that are waveforms constantly changing with time, now positive, now negative. Only at moments of great serenity is it possible to find the pure, the informationless state of signal zero. (p. 404)

A cathode, the negatively charged electrode in a vacuum tube, emits electrons, which pass through the grid to the positively charged plate. Mondaugen thus converts into electronic terms psychological theory (a Freudian notion of the ego as mediator) and philosophical belief in the existence of a timeless self. Here Pynchon accomplishes more than merely displaying his knowledge. It is believable that Mondaugen, an electronics expert who appears in both *V.* and *Gravity's Rainbow*, invents this metaphor. In the former novel he expresses doubts about Weissmann's implication that metaphors have no use in a world composed, as Wittgenstein wrote, of everything that is the case. Moreover, Mondaugen has observed the German racial policy in Southwest Africa and its magnification over a larger area during World War II. That is, his experiences make it natural for him to seek a timeless self, a stable ego, and tranquility.

Critics have often discussed one of the scientific methods of synthesizing data that Pynchon mentions: the concept of entropy. Clausius explained this phenomenon in the Second Law of Thermodynamics, which states that a closed system will always lose energy because its heat will be dissipated. For example, friction will reduce the amount of work that a machine can do. Anne Mangel and others have commented on Pynchon's use of this law, but a few more remarks are needed.[5]

The application of this law to branches of science other than thermodynamics makes interesting material for a novelist. Extending the meaning of this term, Norbert Wiener states, "As entropy increases, the universe, and all closed systems in the universe, tend naturally to deteriorate and lose their distinctiveness, to move from the least to the most probable state, from a state of chaos and sameness" (p. 20). Here Wiener describes the universal behavior of systems by means of a concept that originally described only heat transfer. Entropy thus serves as a widely applicable metaphor. Pynchon uses it to enrich his plot by showing the progressive spreading of chaos, to develop some of his characters by showing their increasing similarity, and to analyze a decaying society.

On the other hand, one can resist or at least avoid entropy. The Second Law of Thermodynamics applies only to closed systems, so open systems can remain free of entropy. Wiener writes that "there are local enclaves whose direction seems opposed to that of the universe at large and in which there is a limited and temporary tendency for organization to increase" (pp. 20–21). Crystals, as Friedman and Puetz indicate, are ordered and enduring, but "brittle and dead" (p. 347). These critics find thirty-five references to crystals in *Gravity's Rainbow*. Love, in contrast, by metaphorically keeping open the boundaries between people, can be both vital and resistant to entropy. Most of Pynchon's characters are closed systems, but a few such a Pökler and Roger Mexico resist the disintegration around them by loving. In addition to love, coherent pattern making fits this description of the non-entropic enclaves or organisms, which are, according to Wiener, "opposed to chaos, to disintegration, to death, as message is to noise" (p. 129). Here, while mentioning death, a prominent feature of all of Pynchon's plots, Wiener says that anything, or any person, who can maintain its organic nature will survive entropy. Wiener thus inadvertently states most of Pynchon's major themes.

To explain Pynchon's novels, critics often cite an early short story, "Entropy," in which some of his later techniques and themes appear in much simpler form. The title, the explicit references to Henry Adams and to entropy, and the characters' actions indicate the importance to this story of Clausius's law. For example, one character, Callisto, fearing that entropy will destroy him, reacts in strange ways, such as keeping constant the temperature of his living quarters. Entropy goes a long way toward explaining the similarity and decadence of the characters and the way these qualities determine the story's plot. A little more subtly, entropy metaphorically describes the plot. For example, a character directs persons arriving at a party to one of a house's two levels and thus works like Maxwell's Demon, another concept related to entropy that plays a part in the novels. James Clerk Maxwell claimed that if a "Demon" sorted into different compartments high-energy particles and low-energy particles the "Demon" could make a perpetual motion machine, because the two compartments would have different amounts of potential energy. As the party in "Entropy" begins to break up, one can see that the people at it lose energy, and they do not move often enough between levels to create perpetual motion, so entropy triumphs.

Pynchon is interested in three of entropy's products: waste, disassembly, and inanimateness. He sometimes uses literal examples of waste as part of a setting, such as the garbage dump where most of "Low-lands" takes place, the sewers in *V.*, and the rubble of the Zone and of London in *Gravity's Rainbow*. The people in Dr. Schoenmaker's waiting room in *V.* have faces nearly equivalent to physical waste. He also uses this concept to describe humans who have metaphorically turned to waste. The connection between literal and metaphoric waste appears in the only essay he has published, a perceptive social analysis, "Journey into the Mind of Watts,"[6] in which he portrays "part of [Watts's] landscape, both the real and the emotional one: busted glass, busted crockery, nails, tin cans, all kinds of scrap and waste" (pp. 148–149). However, as Friedman and Puetz mention, in *Gravity's Rainbow* there are at least seventeen instances of the "compost-garden image" (p. 348), a hybrid image that describes things "that have begun the return to complete disorder and loss of differentiation—to maximum entropy. Yet this collection of the dying is also shown as the garden of birth for life." Thus, Pynchon optimistically, albeit cryptically, implies that entropy can be resisted, that life can triumph.

Critics have commented on Pynchon's many and obvious references to disassembly, but an interesting modulation of tone bears mentioning. Early in *V.* he tells the old joke about the golden screw in the navel. A few pages later when Profane thinks of it and begins to fear his own disassembly, the tone becomes sombre (p. 30). Many pages later the narrator recounts the story of children literally disassembling the Bad Priest, who already had partially turned to waste. By that time disassembly no longer provokes laughter. Several critics have opined that the absence of Slothrop from the last section of *Gravity's Rainbow* is actually a result of his disintegration, metaphoric or literal. That is, these critics think that the surrealistic form of that section—the illogical jamming together of disparate details—imitates Slothrop's personal disintegration and dramatizes both Pynchon's point that the contemporary world is coming apart and his own efforts to hold together the mass of information that he considers pertinent. In any case, a world of difference separates that light hearted joke early in *V.* and the conclusion of *Gravity's Rainbow*, although both develop the theme of disassembly.

Pynchon's theme of inanimateness, especially in *V.*, has been the subject of some critical discussion, but three examples deserve a little more attention. In the first, a jocular one, Pynchon redraws the World War II graffito of Kilroy to make it look like an electronic diagram. The strange branch of psychology that he invents, psychodontics, also qualifies as an example of inanimateness, because it blames human psychological problems on semi-animate teeth. Finally, he proposes a counterforce that will perhaps withstand entropy's impetus toward the inanimate. About a group of people in Southwest Africa the narrator comments, "Community may have been the only solution possible against such an assertion of the Inanimate" (p. 253). German colonial officials there, as Pynchon describes them and as they actually were, considered the natives to be no better than inanimate objects and then by killing them made them literally inanimate.

In *Gravity's Rainbow* a few characters show evidence of genuine inanimateness. One, Tchitcherine, "is more metal than anything else. Steel teeth wink as he talks. Under his pompadour is a silver plate. Gold wirework threads in three-dimensional tattoo among the fine wreckage of cartilage and bone inside his right knee joint" (p. 337). The metaphorically inanimate, however, dominate the *dramatis personae*. As it did in *V.*, vital Africa provides a contrast to them. The Hereros, victims of Germany's Southwest Africa policy, resist inanimateness. Their actions in this novel illustrate an attitude expressed by an actual Herero in a quotation that, whether or not Pynchon read it, certainly fits his conception of these people: "Everyone is greedy. The European is devoted to dead metals. We are more intelligent for we get our joy from living creatures [cattle]."[7]

Another means that scientists use to synthesize data, applying the principle of cause and effect, also interests Pynchon. This traditional method of explanation, despite the attacks by Hume and others, has persisted. It seems innocent enough, merely an epistemological tool, but in *Gravity's Rainbow* Pynchon shows that it has social and psychological concomitants that are far from innocent. Pointsman, the most implacable advocate of cause-and-effect analysis in the book, illustrates these concomitants when he discusses his intellectual hero, Pavlov: " 'His hope was for a long chain of better and better approximations. His faith ultimately lay in a pure physiological basis for the life of the psyche. No effect without cause, and a clear train of linkages' " (p. 89). This kind of analysis is suitable for those who would condition—and thereby control—others. Joseph Slade traces the social and political implications of dependence on cause and effect: "Cause and effect govern the individual and the state. National states or multinational cartels are systems of rationalization, linear networks of 'secular' energies Pynchon identifies with the rise of industrialization. Where one has rationalization, one also has control, the totality of which is measured by the degree to which it represses uncertainty."[8] Edward Mendelson borrows from Max Weber the concept of the routinization of the charismatic to describe effects similar to those mentioned by Slade.[9] Mendelson refers to the rationalization and bureaucratization of irrational and spontaneous forces, a process that he thinks is described again and again in *Gravity's Rainbow*.

Pynchon suggests that, quite apart from its unpleasant political and social implications, cause-and-effect analysis may not adequately explain events and phenomena. For example, this kind of analysis has difficulty with the temporal dislocation that occurs when the rocket breaks the sound barrier and thus arrives before the sound of its approach. This fact merely suggests that cause-and-effect analysis may be flawed, a point that Roger Mexico makes: " 'There's a feeling about that cause-and-effect may have been taken as far as it will go. That for science to carry on at all, it must look for a less narrow, a less . . . sterile set of assumptions' " (p. 89). Pynchon's creating the character of Mexico and indicating the values that go along with his dependence on statistical explanations is a more effective attack on cause-and-effect analysis. Mexico is an "Antipointsman. . . . The young statistician is devoted to number and to method. . . . But in the domain of zero to one, not-something to something, Pointsman can only possess the zero and the one. . . . But to Mexico belongs the domain *between* zero and one—the middle Pointsman has excluded from his persuasion—the probabilities" (p. 55). That is, Mexico deals with percentages, numerical values between zero and one, that calculate the likelihood that an event will occur. By doing so he recognizes that uncertainty is pervasive, that events are random and that anyone trying to understand them can only go so far as quantifying probabilities. Increasing randomness is a feature of the entropic processes that threaten the characters in all of Pynchon's novels, but it also allows for human freedom, for an escape from conditioning. As Lance Ozier puts it, "Mexico can handle (or at least accept) the uncertainty of open personal relationships, while Pointsman must have absolute control over everyone he deals with."[10] Pynchon dramatizes this point when he describes Mexico's relations with others, particularly with Jessica Swanlake.

In addition to its positive aspects, its contrast to the disturbing implications of cause-and-effect analysis, statistics also has its negative side. Pynchon seizes upon the fact that scientists now employ statistics to predict, and in a world full of portents for paranoids, prediction quickly merges with control. Earlier in the history of mechanics simple mathematics sufficed for those who sought to predict physical movement. "According to Newtonian mechanics," claims Jeremy Bernstein, "once the forces and the initial conditions are specified, it is possible to calculate the motions of particles into the indefinite future."[11] Max Planck, Werner Heisenberg, and their followers changed this. Now, contends Erwin Schrödinger, gravitation, the cornerstone of Newton's physics, may be the only physical phenomenon not governed by statistical laws.[12] If Schrödinger can be taken literally, statistical laws apply almost universally and thus Pynchon has good reason to include them in his pervasive theme of control. To look at the bright side, if Schrödinger is correct, gravity escapes the grip of statistics and then the title of Pynchon's most recent novel becomes more significant. Gravity offers a rainbowlike promise of escape at least from prediction and possibly from control.

With the increasing usefulness of statistics has come a new conception of time, which Pynchon adapts for his disjointed plots.[13] Some contemporary scientists have begun to use an alternative to the cause-and-effect epistemology that Mexico suspects, and Leni Pökler believes, is invalid. Considering events in a framework of statistical probability rather than in a cause-

and-effect mold deemphasizes temporal sequences. According to the new concept, events do not happen suddenly and then stop, after which one can determine their causes. Rather, objects persist and change continually as their statistical composition changes. Time then becomes a flux also, because no discrete events divide it into segments. The blurring of causal relationships and the flux produced by rapid shifts in setting and unforeseen turns of events in Pynchon's fiction indicate that the theory of time developed here is this ongoing one rather than the traditional theory that postulates a series of frozen moments that can be distinctly separated and remembered. This new conception of time brings with it important problems, however. For example, one can no longer comfortably believe that he or she and physical events operate in different time sequences; humans now seem to be caught by the kind of time recorded by clocks rather than capable of at least occasionally escaping into timelessness or into a time not divided into equal segments. "Automation," writes Wiener in *Cybernetics*, "exists in the same sort of Bergsonian time as the living organism" (p. 56). This conception of time causes some of the difficulty that Pynchon's characters experience in accommodating themselves to the world of inanimate objects.

Statistics is also connected with the Second Law of Thermodynamics. Callisto in "Entropy" sees the nexus: "It was not, however, until Gibbs and Boltzmann brought to this principle the methods of statistical mechanics that the horrible significance of it all dawned on him: only then did [Callisto] realize that the isolated system—galaxy, engine, human being, culture, whatever—must evolve spontaneously toward the Condition of the Most Probable" (pp. 282–83). The world view Callisto constructs on the basis of this realization explains the desperate measures he takes. One must recognize that this view is Callisto's alone. The norm in this story as well as in the rest of Pynchon's work approximates the opposite theory that the improbable dominates.

Several times in *Gravity's Rainbow* Pynchon mentions a major statistical tool of prediction, the Poisson distribution. For example, it accurately predicts the fall of bombs on London, thus explaining a major part of the plot to the characters who know

about it. Later, a much less orthodox method of prediction proves
just as effective; a map of Slothrop's sexual activities reveals
where the bombs will fall. One scientist attributes this correlation
to precognition and another attributes it to psychokinesis, but
Roger Mexico, who had believed that statistics explains
everything, merely evades the issue by calling the correlation a
statistical oddity (p. 85). More likely, it represents a triumph of the
human over the numerical. Because of Slothrop's map, Mexico's
faith in mathematics crumbles slightly, preparing him for the
tender relation he establishes later with Jessica Swanlake, thereby
escaping the war's horrors. A correlation that begins as a joke and
an occasion to display still more erudition thus plays an
important part in the development of one of this novel's few
changing characters. By breaking the cycle of obsessive scientists
predicting the results of other obsessive scientists' work, the
usefulness of Slothrop's map also contributes to the thematic
statement about the limitations of scientific ways of organizing
information.

Pynchon presents another alternative to cause-and-effect
analysis. In one scene the contrast is direct, created by describing
an interaction between two characters who have adopted two
different methods of analysis. While watching a movie, Franz
Pökler alternately falls asleep and awakens. His wife Leni
comments, " 'You're the cause-and-effect man'. . . . How did
he connect together the fragments he saw while his eyes were
open?" (p. 159). In turn, he attacks her belief in astrology, which
she defends by denying the validity of cause-and-effect analysis.
She explains that astrology does not seek causes: " 'It all goes
along together. Parallel, not series. Metaphor. Signs and
symptoms. Mapping on to different coordinate systems' " (p.
159). In her reply, one of this novel's most important passages,
Pynchon justifies many of his fictional techniques: his creation of
metaphors and analogies, his exploration of the occult and other
strange explanatory systems, and, in general, his pattern making.
Pynchon later calls Pökler an extension of the rocket, although
that character's tender encounters with his daughter eventually
change his mechanistic outlook. The dependence of the rocket
engineers on cause-and-effect analysis signifies for Pynchon the

strategy of trying to overcome the rocket by identifying and exemplifying an alternative epistemological assumption.

In contrast to the analysts of causes and effects, "those like Slothrop, with the greatest interest in discovering the truth, were thrown back on dreams, psychic flashes, omens, cryptographies, drug-epistemologies, all dancing on a ground of terror, contradiction, absurdity" (p. 582.). This alternate epistemology creates dangerous possibilities, in addition to offering a chance to discover truth. In this quotation Pynchon identifies the reason for his many descriptions of drug use: the users are trying, among other things, to escape science and its assumptions. Pynchon's scientists and his "dopers" continually confront each other, a natural situation because the dopers' drugs are the products of organic chemistry: they use some of the same substances that the scientists use for synthesis. Among the confrontations are the competition between rocket scientists and cocaine users for potassium permanganate. Also, some of the scientists invade the dopers' realm by seeking a non-addictive analgesic drug similar to morphine (p. 348). The dopers, however, can take comfort because a crucial event in the history of organic chemistry, Kekulé's discovery of the shape of the benzene molecule, happened during a dream. That is, many of the developments in this branch of science depend not on scientific reasoning but on an insight arrived at through the drugs-dreams-occult method of thinking.

Like the Second Law of Thermodynamics and cause-and-effect epistemology, the new science of cybernetics plays an important role in Pynchon's work. Norbert Wiener, the most important cyberneticist, defines this science as the "field of control and communication theory, whether in the machine or in the animal."[14] Later cyberneticists have accepted this definition and have used it to guide their inquiries. Porter's book on the subject, which appeared twenty-one years after Wiener's, defines cybernetics virtually the same way: "the science of control and communication in man and machine" (p. 19). These definitions show the wide applicability of cybernetics, its usefulness, and the qualities about it that disturb Pynchon. A good deal of life, both human and nonhuman, falls under the aegis of control and communication. Cybernetics has two particularly frightening implications. The resemblance of innocuous communication to insidious control would worry any prudent person and would terrify anyone with paranoid tendencies. Also, the power gained by acquiring information both promises self-liberation and suggests that whoever controls information and communication controls people.

Cybernetics, more clearly than other sciences, organizes disparate kinds of information. At a key moment in its history a cyberneticist recognized that the equation for information loss duplicates the equation for entropy, which encouraged Wiener and his associates to believe that they could find general laws, widely applicable investigatory techniques, and similarities among the sciences. That is, the early cyberneticists dreamed of devising a new science that would combine parts of the old sciences by arranging information into new meaningful patterns. Developments in computer science have aided their efforts, and they have pointed out striking analogies among sciences. Even our language, because of its cybernetic jargon, such as "feed-back," shows their influence. Further extension into the social sciences followed in such works as Wiener's later, less technical book *The Human Use of Human Beings*. He identifies his interests in its subtitle, *Cybernetics and Society*, and in some of its chapter titles, such as "The Mechanism and History of Language," "Law and Communication" and "Communication, Secrecy and Social Policy." In another of his books, *God and Golem*, Wiener extends his ideas even further from their source into religion. Occasionally the cyberneticists explain nonscientific phenomena too simply and less revealingly than traditional scientists do, but they do have exciting goals and offer many new insights.

Like most of the other kinds of science in Pynchon's books, particularly in *Gravity's Rainbow*, cybernetics developed rapidly during World War II. In fact, this science began then, with efforts to improve anti-aircraft defense, and it grew partly because of developments in radar. In other words, cybernetics at first was a counterforce to the rocket. Arthur Porter enumerates the main contributions of World War II technology to control science, the field that includes cybernetics: (1) servomechanisms for computers, radar, and armaments (devices in which one part repeats with increased power another part's motion), (2) precision-control devices that can use impure data (data-filtering mechanisms), which have improved nuclear reactors, chemical plants, and apparatuses for tracking satellites, (3) the construction of servomechanisms from standard building blocks, which has aided the development of systems analysis, (4) studies of man-machine systems, such as radar and computers, which have spawned human factors engineering (pp. 77–78).

Because cyberneticists owe many of their insights to computer science, they have contemplated the meanings and uses of the binary system of numbers. Analogue computers, such as the slide rule, are based on spatial relationships and continua rather than on dichotomies. The more common digital computers, however, are based on the binary system, which is constructed on the base two, and operate by choosing between only two alternatives in each instance, although the number of pairs they work with may be enormous. That is, proponents of the binary system, such as Pointsman, choose between one and zero and ignore all the values in between. The binary system creates a new framework, a scientific context, in which to place old dualistic notions. Dualism can form the basis of a cosmology and, as dialectic, can be part of an epistemology, but Pynchon's characters view this feature of computers merely as threatening and limiting. McClintic Sphere in *V.* learns about a primitive kind of computer:

> He had found out from this sound man about a two-triode circuit called a flip-flop, which when it was turned on could be one of two ways, depending on which tube was conducting and which was cut off: set or reset, flip or flop.
> "And that," the man said, "can be yes or no, or one or zero. And that is what you might call one of the basic units, or specialized 'cells' in a big 'electronic brain.' " (p. 273)

Sphere considers this dualism unacceptable and immediately propounds his advice about keeping cool but caring, in which he tries to articulate a way of behaving that avoids unattractive opposites.

Like Sphere, Oedipa Maas recoils at computerlike dualism; she is "waiting for a symmetry of choices to break down" (p. 136). A little later she actually equates her limited range of choices with that of a computer: "It was now like walking among matrices of a great digital computer, the zeroes and ones twinned above" (p. 136). She fears that she must choose between the Tristero, which may not even exist, and the reality of San Narciso, the well-named California city in which she lives. Her abhorrence of both possibilities militates against reading *The Crying of Lot 49* merely as social criticism opposing everything San Narciso represents and supporting an alternative system, represented by the Tristero but having any identity that a reader wishes to give it. This scene also reveals Oedipa's intellectual limits in her inability to escape dualism. One sees here a possible reason for this entrapment by dualism: the computer's pervasive influence. Oedipa never escapes from these limits. At the end of the novel, only two pages after the passage just quoted, she still hopefully awaits an answer.

In *Gravity's Rainbow* Pynchon uses dualism less in themes than in characterization, especially in his doubles. Two pages before Blicero speculates on doubles, his own double, Enzian, discusses unification of opposites: "To the boy Ndjambi Karunga is what happens when they couple, that's all: God is creator and destroyer, sun and darkness, all sets of opposites brought together, including black and white, male and female" (p. 100). That is, sex can unite opposites. In these terms Blicero's strange homosexual attachment to Enzian makes sense. Although not realistic—after all, they are a Nazi and a Black—this relationship develops the theme of dualism. It also helps explain why many of Pynchon's characters try to find meaning in heterosexual relations. If dualism plagues the world and the most obvious resolution of opposites occurs between men and women, sex is probably a way to escape dualism. Variations on the usual sexual arrangement, such as Blicero and Enzian's relationship, give the characters at least a chance to avoid dualism, if not to transcend it. A few of the heterosexual relationships, however, such as Roger Mexico and Jessica Swanlake's, offer the most hope.

Anne Mangel writes a clear introduction to cybernetic theories of information, even though her article covers only *The Crying of Lot 49*. She presents the equation for entropy (Boltzmann's) and its twin, the equation for information (Shannon's). The former is

$$H = -\sum_{j} \text{pj log pj}$$

Where H = entropy

The latter is

$$\text{average information/symbol} = -\sum \text{pj log pj}$$

(p. 202)

She clearly explains Maxwell's Demon, with the useful reminder that it works because it has certain information, which implies that by obtaining information one can resist entropy. This fact about the Demon fits the plots and themes of *The Crying of Lot 49* and of the two other novels. Mangel also shows how scientific theories influence Pynchon's elements of fiction. For example, she writes that "the notion of information being altered and lost in the process of transmission is found throughout *The Crying of Lot 49*," and she cites several examples (p.204). A finer distinction becomes necessary at this point: it is the characters, not Pynchon, who transmit information badly.

Before further considering cybernetics' organization of information, one needs to see how it defines information. According to Robert W. Marks, information "is observable pattern."[15] "Significant information," he continues, "is a report, interpreted in some specific context, of a change of state that has occurred somewhere" (p. 232). Although set in a scientific context, these definitions perfectly suit a novelist. Marks's emphasis on pattern fits the notion of literature as a way of organizing information. This definition of significant information recalls the way in which a novelist arranges the other elements of his fiction around the central core of his plot, which reports on changes of state.

The cyberneticists know, of course, that scientists have not preempted information gathering. To the contrary, acquisition and distribution of information, they think, form the basis of society. "The social system," Wiener states in *Cybernetics*, "is an organization like the individual . . . it is bound together by a system of communication . . . it has a dynamics, in which circular processes of a feedback nature play an important part" (p. 33). If Wiener has properly constructed this model of society, epistemological problems often cause social problems. Earlier he makes clear the "dynamics" of society. The identity of Boltzmann's and Shannon's equations allows Wiener to claim that "just as the amount of information in a system is a measure of its degree of organization, so the entropy of a system is a measure of its degree of disorganization" (p. 18). In these terms society is the battleground where the forces of information battle the forces of entropy. The disorganized societies that Pynchon describes lose energy and sink toward inertness, thereby forcing their members to grasp desperately for bits of information.

In *The Human Use of Human Beings* Wiener expands on the last quotation cited, writing that "it is the thesis of this book that society can only be understood through a study of the messages and the communication facilities which belong to it" (p. 25). His use of "only" causes an overstatement, but he enunciates an interesting conception of society. Logically, one would expect change also in the literary genre supposedly most attuned to social changes. Present confusion about the novel's relation to society often makes it difficult for readers to understand contemporary fiction. Wiener's conception of society and the discoveries of his fledgling science provide one means of understanding some contemporary novels. Pynchon certainly makes good sense in cybernetic terms because of both his descriptions of communication and his own unusual, sophisticated communications.

Cyberneticists recognize that even successfully coping with the enormous amount of available information will not immediately create a utopia. Another problem arises from bad information, which they call noise, their word choice reflecting again their science's origin in electronics. In addition, lost information creates further problems. Saul in "Entropy" and the Hereros in *Gravity's Rainbow* agonize over the latter difficulty. Saul worries about the ambiguity of "I love you." The Hereros attribute much of their agony to the messages they have not received, so they search for the rocket, hoping that it will provide the answers that they lack. Oedipa Maas tries even harder to compensate for lost information. She sometimes considers the Tristero to be a system in which people are "truly communicating whilst reserving their lies, recitations of routine, arid betrayals of spiritual poverty, for the official government delivery system" (p. 128). The Tristero remains so shadowy, even its existence being open to question, that this statement should be taken to reveal her yearnings rather than Pynchon's alarm over social lies, his desire for social alternatives, and his conception of those alternatives.

Because of information's social and personal importance, one must know how to obtain it. From Marks's definition of information as observable patterns it follows that learning consists of recognizing patterns. Porter agrees: "Patterns that are probabilistic . . . are the basis of learning in all its forms, of discovering and of creating" (p. 143). One needs to discover patterns not only when one has too little information but also when one has too much. Pynchon's characters find themselves in the latter difficulty much more often than in the former. The more Oedipa learns about Pierce Inverarity's empire, for example, the less effectively can she order her knowledge and the less capably can she act. Herbert Stencil experiences the same difficulties while he gathers information about V. In the preface to Porter's book Marshall McLuhan mentions this difficulty: "The speed-up of information movement creates an environment of 'information overload' that demands pattern recognition for human survival" (p. v).

An important part of cybernetics' information theory concerns feedback. The most important kind, negative feedback, reports on the difference between desired and actual behavior. The etymology of the word *cybernetics* reveals the importance of negative feedback. This science's name derives from the Greek word for steersman. Whoever named it probably thought of a steersman constantly checking the position of the rudder (the actual behavior) against the course (the desired behavior). Electronics experts and cyberneticists employed the concept of feedback for a long time before bureaucrats appropriated the word and added their meaning to it. Scientists have used this concept to clarify important issues. For example, Porter asserts that learning is a feedback process (p. 148). That is, in order to learn, one needs to keep trying to fit new data into patterns already formed and to keep measuring one's success. Like many of the cyberneticists' other concepts, this one helps to explain Pynchon's work; as he writes he continually ramifies patterns that he has already established.

Pynchon integrates oscillation, another phenomenon explained by cybernetics, into his work so completely that he hides its relation to that science. Mishandling or overloading will cause yawing (wild oscillation) in a mechanism that responds to feedback. For instance, if a rocket wanders too far from its correct orbit, constant signals to its feedback mechanism can cause yawing. Unchecked positive feedback will produce the same effect. "Positive" in this case means duplicated or reinforced, not desirable. Positive feedback is cumulative and theoretically can be infinite. For example, if a microphone receives from a speaker sound that it had sent out itself, positive feedback will result. This effect resembles a series of reflections in two mirrors that face each other.

Pynchon alludes to feedback in several different ways. In *V.* there is a strange clock in the office of Esther's plastic surgeon:

> The pendulum didn't swing back and forth but was in the form of a disc, parallel to the floor and driven by a shaft which paralleled the hands at six o'clock. The disc turned a quarter-revolution one way, then a quarter-revolution the other, each reversed torsion on the shaft advancing the escapement a notch. Mounted on the disc were two imps or demons, wrought in gold, posed in fantastic attitudes. Their movements were reflected in the mirror along with the window at Rachel's back, which extended from floor to ceiling and revealed the branches and green needles of a pine tree. The branches whipped back and forth in the February wind, ceaseless and shimmering. (p. 35)

Many things lie under the surface of this precise description. Later the writer himself draws some inferences from it, but he does not mention oscillation. The moving disc of course oscillates, and, less obviously, the mirror and the window, which reflect under certain conditions of light, can create positive feedback ad infinitum. The wind also causes positive feedback and makes the trees outside oscillate "ceaselessly." The mirror and the window reflect the disc and trees, thereby tying together the three oscillations and piling infinity on infinity. In addition to its cleverness, the scene perfectly fits Esther's oscillation. The "negative feedback" caused by the disparity between her actual and desired conditions "overloads" her so that she can barely cope. She has come to this office for plastic surgery and, although she does not know it, she will soon begin an unfortunate affair with her doctor.

A few pages earlier in *V.* oscillation occurs on a planetary scale: "If you look from the side at a planet swinging around in its orbit, split the sun with a mirror and imagine a string, it all looks like a yo-yo. The point furthest from the sun is called aphelion. The point furthest from the yo-yo hand is called, by analogy, apocheir" (p. 26). This optical trick makes the planet's orbit appear to be not an ellipse but a straight-line oscillation between the aphelion and the apocheir. Some of the characters in *V.* feel compelled to oscillate like this planet for long periods of time. They even call this activity yo-yoing. Besides being an apt trope, "yo-yo" is a pun on "yaw." One page after the optical trick described in the quotation just cited, the narrator says that "Profane woke up early, couldn't get back to sleep and decided on a whim to spend the day like a yo-yo, shuttling on the subway back and forth underneath 42nd Street, from Times Square to Grand Central and vice versa" (p. 27). Critics have often mentioned this passage and others about yo-yoing as examples of the aimlessness and ennui that afflict many characters in this novel, but its relation to negative feedback has not been explicated. Pynchon names the Yoyodyne Company in *The Crying of Lot 49* after this same phenomenon, although no one connected with this company knows that its name comments on its aimless and uncontrollably repetitive work.

Pynchon introduces his theme of control, which is important to cyberneticists, early in *Gravity's Rainbow*. At a séance the medium speaks in terms applicable to a rocket: " 'All these things arise from one difficulty: control. For the first time it was *inside*, do you see. The control is put inside. No more need to suffer

passively under "outside forces"—to veer into any wind' " (p. 30).
Then he makes an analogy: " 'A market needed no longer be run
by the Invisible Hand, but now could *create itself*—its own logic,
momentum, style, from *inside*' " (p. 30). A few pages earlier
Pynchon had described a Puritan gravestone, and the juxtaposition of these passages suggests that the doctrine of predestination
can be conceived as a matter of inside control. Historical,
psychological, and many other kinds of phenomena discussed in
this novel also relate to the theme of control. Human freedom, its
possibilities and limits, is one of his major topics. However, the
chance remains, as the medium soon points out, that control is
merely an illusion, and this possibility disturbs rather than
comforts some of the characters.

Pynchon also dramatizes an interesting psychological
phenomenon based on the relationship between knowledge and
control. If knowledge allows control over others, lack of
knowledge allows control by others. Certain from the beginning
that they lack information, his characters feel that something
controls them, even though they cannot identify that thing. Thus,
lack of information combined with failure to discover the cause of
this predicament creates paranoia. Again, epistemological issues
form a foundation, this time of the dominant psychological
disability in his work. In his novels occur dozens of connections
between lack of information and paranoia. One of the most
poignant, in *Gravity's Rainbow*, concerns Katje. She does not
know what has happened to Blicero, whom she had loved, so she
imagines his destiny and thereby reveals her paranoid symptoms:
"He's gone beyond *his* pain, *his* sin—driven deep into Their
province, into control, synthesis and control" (p. 661).

In addition to the technological control of objects, Pynchon
describes the social control of people. This social criticism
usually is very clear, except for one aspect. Some of the strangest
scenes in *Gravity's Rainbow*, as well as some of the most moving,
comment on social control. Many of the baffling scenes are
variations on the theme of minority tastes. That is, they describe
powerless characters who have developed bizarre tastes in order to
create a small area of their lives where they can resist the control of
the powerful. Many characters, for example, have minority tastes
in sex, which Pynchon describes vividly and exhaustively.

Strange eating habits recounted in such scenes as the opening, where characters devour bananas prepared in an endless variety of ways, and the scene about exotic and unappetizing candy also develop this theme of resistance to control. Other characters idiosyncratically prefer Rossini to Beethoven and the kazoo to more conventional instruments.

Although cybernetics furnishes no symbol as meaningful as the rocket in *Gravity's Rainbow*, it plays a role at least as important in Pynchon's books as that of any other branch of science. Its efforts to deal with information make this science particularly relevant to his work. It both combines bits of other sciences and applies scientific ideas to nonscientific phenomena, as Pynchon performs a syncretic function, especially by finding literary uses for nonliterary concepts and images. This field may not offer the best explanation of contemporary society, but Pynchon has effectively used some of its insights, and he cannot be fully understood without tracing the influence of cybernetics on his work.

Mathematics is the other synthetic scientific discipline that figures prominently in Pynchon's fiction. By drawing non-mathematical conclusions from mathematics and by incorporating it into his literary works, he points out a feature that its useful technological applications might easily obscure: mathematics is metaphoric because it describes universals. Along these lines, Arthur Porter writes in *Cybernetics Simplified* that "metaphor in science is synonymous with the physical and mathematical model" (p. 79). In fact, mathematics sometimes proceeds a long distance from observable reality and appears virtually useless. But its universality is also its chief virtue and the reason for its usefulness. Sometimes its utility is obscured and its discoveries lie dormant, waiting to be applied, as Riemann's geometry did until Einstein needed it.

Pynchon also assesses mathematical ways of organizing information. The mathematical foundations of modern science alone justify such attention, for mathematics orders the physical sciences and some parts of the biological sciences. On a more pragmatic level Pynchon clarifies the effect that mathematics has had on commonsense notions. Systems based on mathematics have of course also played an important part in the history of western philosophy since Pythagoras argued that the universe manifests the principles of Number. This fact, too, makes valuable Pynchon's analysis of mathematical thought. In the seventeenth century, for example, when revolutionary scientific developments excited philosophers, mathematical philosophy was dominant. Some twentieth-century philosophers, such as Whitehead and Russell, have been mathematicians, but these two built their philosophies on other foundations.

In the century when mathematical philosophy was most important, Pascal's early work on conic sections led him to extend geometrical concepts into other realms of thought. Conic sections are important to *Gravity's Rainbow* because one of them, the parabola, describes the rocket's flight. In this novel the rocket represents, among other things, the triumph of mathematics; yet one must remember that, to use Pascal's term, *l'esprit de finesse* of Pynchon launched it. Another major thinker of the seventeenth century, Spinoza, made perhaps even greater use of mathematics in his philosophy, although, unlike Pascal, he made no contributions to mathematics. In his *Ethics* he employs a geometrical form and method of reasoning. Like Pascal, he looked to mathematics for general, clear, and accurate philosophical knowledge. Unlike Pascal, he seems to be only implicitly relevant to *Gravity's Rainbow*.

The other important seventeenth-century mathematical philosopher and co-inventor of calculus, Leibnitz, becomes relevant to *Gravity's Rainbow* when two characters jointly discover that the Germans have built the tunnels of the rocket facilities at Nordhausen in the shape of the SS emblem and the double integral sign (p. 300). More than an interesting but trivial juxtaposition, this information helps explain a mental attitude that underlies much of the novel's action. Pynchon suggests that the reductiveness of mathematics is similar to that exemplified by the Nazis' dehumanization of others, which allowed them to commit atrocities. If one can conceive of rocketry merely as a mathematical problem, for instance, one can fire rockets against a civilian population. Pynchon sets down several equations involved in rocketry to show that one can consider warfare in such sterile, detached terms. Later he makes the same point more explicitly: "film and calculus, both pornographies of flight. Reminders of impotence and abstraction" (p. 567). The double integral also signifies distancing, moving away twice from the entity with which one begins, and suggests dehumanization. Leibnitz had a sensibility that allowed him both to be one of the founders of calculus and to defend the position that the world, including its evil, is the way it must be. In other words, he could manipulate and distance reality by means of mathematics, and he could similarly justify any kind of evil by distancing it and considering it as part of a cosmic system. Leibnitz belongs to the German intellectual tradition that Pynchon, looking back from a postwar vantage point, tries to understand and to which, one can often infer, he ascribes some of the blame for World War II.

As Lance Ozier has discovered, Pynchon uses a cluster of mathematical images to make an important thematic point in *Gravity's Rainbow*.[16] Ozier notes several references in the novel to Δt, such as "Δt approaching zero, eternally approaching, the slices of time growing thinner and thinner" (pp. 158–59). For Leni Pökler, the speaker of those words, contends Ozier, this symbol "signified a transcendent pure present incarnate at the moment of personal commitment" (p. 197). Similarly, he continues, the double integral sign represents time dissolving into eternity. He also considers that the Brennschluss Point, the point where the rocket begins its downward flight, marks a transformation into a new order. He generalizes that "in the novel's terms the two worlds or states separated by the Δt/Brennschluss Point/singular point experience seem to be the world of cause-and-effect populated by the Elect and its bureaucracies and a transcendent, atemporal realm of uncircumscribed potential which nevertheless is grounded in the former world and is therefore not pure chaos" (p. 203).

In another revealing comparison Pynchon maps mathematics onto the flow of history: "If tensor analysis is good enough for turbulence, it ought to be good enough for history. There ought to be nodes, critical points . . . there ought to be super-derivatives of the crowded and insatiate flow that can be set equal to zero and these critical points found" (p. 451). Tensor analysis, the branch of mathematics used to determine the position of something when more than one system of coordinates is applicable, has a prominent place in rocketry. It must be used to predict a trajectory, because the firing impetus, yaw, gravity, and other forces that affect motion each has its own system of coordinates. In other ways, too, Pynchon combines history and mathematics. For example, he mentions in *Gravity's Rainbow* that at a cusp infinite speed in one direction changes to infinite speed in the opposite direction (p. 664). Similarly, in certain eras history's movement in one direction stops and one set of coordinates (such as a war) reverses it. Furthermore, he uses this notion of critical points in history in *V.* and *Gravity's Rainbow*, where he concentrates on, and thereby suggests the great influence of, a few crucial eras.

In *Gravity's Rainbow* Pynchon interrupts a description of a sadomasochistic orgy to use mathematical information in an improbable way. After mentioning the point at the top of a woman's stocking, he suddenly mentions "a cosmology: of nodes and cusps and points of osculation. . . . Consider cathedral spires, holy minarets, the crunch of trainwheels over the points . . . even, according to the Russian mathematician Friedmann, the infinitely dense point from which the present Universe expanded" (p. 396). Like nodes, the other two mathematical terms refer to points where curves double back on themselves.

Mathematical information clarifies the major symbol in *Gravity's Rainbow*. On the one hand, the rocket ramifies into dozens of symbolic meanings but, on the other, its path can be expressed by a simple mathematical equation. As to its symbolic meanings, at times in this book Pynchon is almost literally accurate when he writes that "everything, always, collectively, had been moving toward that purified shape latent in the sky" (p. 209). As to mathematics, the rainbow of the novel's title alludes to the rocket's parabolic flight, which can be represented by the following graph and equations:

$x = vt \cos \alpha$ $y = vt \sin \alpha + 1/2\ gt^2$
g (acceleration) is constant if air resistance is neglected.
v = initial velocity in ft/sec.

Of course, such bland precision does not comfort the people on whom the rockets fall.

The mathematics of rocketry also depends a good deal on Newton's work, and so older scientific information plays a role in *Gravity's Rainbow*, even though newer information such as that discovered by Einstein and Heisenberg has had more impact on contemporary literature as a whole and on other fields. Newton, explains Jeremy Bernstein in his book on Einstein, "was able to show . . . that the only possible particle orbits for one particle moving under the gravitational influence of another . . . are conic sections. Which of these orbits a particle selects depends on . . . how much initial velocity is given to it" (pp. 29–30). Thus, the mathematical work of Pascal and of others who followed Einstein's lead suddenly became much more important. "All of this," Bernstein continues, "has now become very familiar from rocketry." Indeed, and Pynchon's development of the rocket as a symbol has helped to make it familiar.

Pynchon, then, is not a frustrated scientist merely leaving shards of scientific information strewn around in his novels, particularly in *Gravity's Rainbow*. He assembles these shards, impressive enough individually, into a vessel both beautiful and, because it orders and thus explains the world around it, useful. The glue he uses is a contrast made by Pascal, whose work exhibits a major tension between *l'esprit geometrique* and *l'esprit de finesse*. The geometrical spirit of the scientists and of the characters who think like them bears major responsibility for the war in *Gravity's Rainbow*. It also opposes a more dexterous and free-wheeling spirit embodied by a few characters and even more by Pynchon's own literary prestidigitations.

3.

Psychology

In addition to his easily noticed and often comic descriptions of eccentric characters, Pynchon undertakes more scholarly tasks: he presents considerable raw information about human psychological traits. The most common negative traits of his characters—paranoia, aggression, and anality—stand in the way of their achieving mature love, the most important positive trait he depicts. He does not stop with this traditional psychological analysis of characters. Rather, he goes on to demonstrate how psychological information is integrated by several psychological schools: Freudianism (including Erik Erikson and Norman O. Brown), gestalt psychology (represented by Wolfgang Köhler), Jungianism, and the behaviorism of I.P. Pavlov.

Of the three negative traits on which Pynchon concentrates, paranoia is the most important. According to him, two of its symptoms relate to information: belief that one has secret information and fear that one lacks important information that someone else knows. As to the former, old Godolphin in *V.* thinks that "below the glittering integument of every foreign land there is a hard dead-point of truth and that in all cases—even England's—it is the same kind of truth, can be phrased in identical words" (p. 169). Weissmann's belief in secret signals from outer space can also be interpreted as evidence of paranoia.

In contrast, a big question, succinctly stated in *Gravity's Rainbow*, haunts people who exhibit the other symptom and are tormented by the question "What *is* it they know that the powerless do not?" (p. 165).

At one point Pynchon suggests several cures for paranoia. In *The Crying of Lot 49* when Oedipa decides that an evil force may be opposing her, the narrator mentions some possible responses: "She may fall back on superstition, or take up a useful hobby like embroidery, or go mad, or marry a disk jockey" (p. 11). In jocular terms, this passage enumerates the major alternatives to which the characters turn again and again. Some, such as the Hereros, are superstitious; others modify this strategy to construct more viable and sophisticated systems of belief. Hobbies or occupations more complicated than embroidery, such as building a rocket, temporarily work for other people. By now it should be clear that many of the characters go mad. Others change the last alternative to genuine love and thereby survive.

As his career has developed, Pynchon in two important ways has changed his conception of paranoia. First, he has treated with increasing seriousness the possibility that evil plots do in fact exist and that therefore paranoids are right, not sick. In his early short story "The Secret Integration" he creates sympathy for the plotting of some children, thereby suggesting that plots can be benign. Disturbed by the iniquities of the adults in their small town, the children seek escape. Eight-year-old Hogan Slothrop, Tyrone Slothrop's brother, becomes an alcoholic. Most of his friends resist the adults by forming Spartacus, a secret conspiracy that annually directs Operation A against the adults. The wild imaginativeness and youth of the plotters make them appear comic, but a sombre tone takes over when they temporarily stop plotting and participate in the town's normal life. In each of Pynchon's first two novels only one person believes in a plot seriously enough to try wholeheartedly to understand it. Furthermore, in *V.* the narrator and sometimes even Stencil himself doubt that a plot exists. The former once reports, "Stencil sketched the entire history of V. that night and strengthened a long suspicion. That it did add up only to the recurrence of an initial and a few dead objects" (p. 419). Stencil admits that " 'V.'s is a country of coincidence, ruled by a ministry of myth' " (p. 423). By creating only one believer in plots Pynchon emphasizes the mental state of the searcher and deemphasizes the possibility of a plot. In *Gravity's Rainbow*, however, many characters join the search, and the suspected plot is more likely to exist and more important.

Second, Pynchon also makes it seem more likely that a larger plot exists behind the smaller one to which the characters direct their attention. Although he usually seeks only V., Stencil occasionally considers the possibility that "his quarry fitted in with The Big One, the century's master cabal" (p. 210). Early in her search Oedipa decides that the Tristero may be only a smokescreen hiding Pierce Inverarity's much larger plot. She cannot solve the mysteries of the little plot, much less those of the big plot. In *Gravity's Rainbow* people trying to find the rocket create their own secret intelligence-gathering plots, and some soon discover evidence that a secret international cartel of industrialists may control the rocket builders. Like the other development, this one indicates Pynchon's increasing desire to examine the possibility that the paranoids are correct.

In various ways he relates paranoia to social and aesthetic matters. He presents its characteristic forms in various societies; for example, in Puritan England belief in predestination often shaded into paranoia. One Puritan, Robert Scurvham, Pynchon reports in *The Crying of Lot 49*,

> had founded during the reign of Charles I, a sect of most pure Puritans. Their central hangup had to do with predestination. There were two kinds. Nothing for a Scurvhamite ever happened by accident. Creation was a vast, intricate machine. But one part of it, the Scurvhamite part, ran off the will of God, its prime mover. The rest ran off some opposite Principle, something blind, soulless; a brute automatism that led to eternal death (p. 116).

Oedipa thinks she discovers relations between the Tristero and these Puritans. In *Gravity's Rainbow* Pynchon describes "a Puritan reflex of seeking other orders behind the visible, also known as paranoia" (p. 188). Because the Puritans were very influential in shaping American society, the persistence of

American paranoia should surprise no one. It has, however, become secularized and transmuted into political forms, such as a group similar to the John Birch Society that appears in *The Crying of Lot 49*. These people, the Peter Pinguid Society, find their inspiration and the justification for their right-wing politics in a naval hero who supposedly withstood the Russians during the Civil War. This group attacks industrialism, a position supported by a vast amount of evidence in *Gravity's Rainbow*, but, much less credibly, they also believe that the John Birch Society is too far to the Left. Pynchon's satire of them contrasts with his occasional suggestions that the paranoid view of a situation can reveal more of the truth than a "normal" view can.

The first of Pynchon's paranoids is Irving Loon, an Ojibwa, who appears in his first published work, a little-known short story, "Mortality and Mercy in Vienna." For two reasons Loon probably deserves more pity than any other of Pynchon's characters. First, he literally is paranoid; the story ends with his firing an automatic rifle into the crowd at a party. Second, his society has made it virtually certain that he will become a paranoid. Their poverty makes starvation the dominant fact of the Ojibwas' lives. Always in trouble, they understandably follow a tribal custom by believing in the existence of many evil spirits. Because of their belief, as well as hallucinations caused by starvation and their cultural conditioning, they also believe in the Windigo: a giant, destructive skeleton composed of ice. During this stage of the typical Ojibwa paranoia the Indian's perceptions alter, he begins to believe that people near him are animals, and he becomes capable of cannibalism. Although a very great generalization is required to do so, one can plausibly argue that the Ojibwa culture as a whole is paranoid. Because this argument makes considerable sense and since this story is Pynchon's first, "Mortality and Mercy in Vienna" offers important clues to his later work, which portrays other somewhat paranoid societies, including our own.

The foreign society that many people would consider paranoid, whether or not they have read Pynchon, is Nazi Germany. Some have claimed that Germany during that era exhibited a national neurosis, the claims ranging in subtlety from

World War II propaganda such as Richard M. Brickner's *Is Germany Incurable?* to Fromm's *Escape from Freedom* and other sophisticated books. Pynchon begins to depict Germany's mental condition in *The Crying of Lot 49* by creating a stereotyped ex-Nazi scientist, the psychoanalyst Dr. Hilarius. Convinced that They are not only after him but also are closing in, he goes berserk and barricades himself in his office. *Gravity's Rainbow* as well includes many bits of evidence of Germany's possible paranoia.

Pynchon's most important comparison between art and paranoia derives from his recognition that both artists and paranoids construct patterns out of information. An artist presents a multitude of facts, characters, actions, and ideas, gradually clarifying the interrelations among them. The paranoid's obsession with meaning compels him to make similar connections. How, then, do writers and paranoids differ? Both deal with many of the same bits of information, so it will not help to begin with the general distinction that a writer creates an imaginary world whereas a paranoid tries to understand the real world. Moreover, Pynchon continually shows, through the elements of his fiction, that one cannot directly understand the real world. One can begin more effectively to contrast paranoid and literary patterns by saying that in general artists give more aesthetically pleasing form to data than do non-artists, although the results may not be more helpful. Artists can accomplish this partly because they know that they construct fictions—and some, such as Pynchon, have impressive insights into the nature of fictions—but paranoids believe that their strange patterns accurately and directly depict reality.

Occasionally Pynchon explicitly compares literary and nonliterary patterns of information, sometimes showing that the nonliterary ones are tinctured with paranoia. For example, in *The Crying of Lot 49* amidst all of Oedipa's efforts to order the bizarre details that rush at her, a pattern connects two levels of reality, as opposed to a pattern existing only on the level of Oedipa's action. The play within the novel, *The Courier's Tragedy*, occupies another level of reality, since according to this novel's norms it is fictive, a work of art contrasted with the actions that are, again according to this novel's norms, real. Then the pattern begins to take shape. The Tristero lurks in the play's background, though textual problems about an important line obfuscate its meaning and its relation to the main plot. In both the play and the main plot line characters learn about the bones of murdered men lying at the bottom of a lake. According to the play's plot summary, "Angelo, then, evil Duke of Squamuglia, has perhaps ten years before the play's opening murdered the good Duke of adjoining Faggio, by poisoning the feet on an image of Saint Narcissus, Bishop of Jerusalem, in the court chapel, which feet the Duke was in the habit of kissing every Sunday at Mass" (p. 45). Two threads connect this passage to the rest of the plot. Oedipa lives in San Narciso, and early in the novel her husband whistles a popular song, "I Want to Kiss Your Feet." Because of these connections, in the novel "reality" begins to imitate art, thus suggesting that it is not unquestionably more real than art.

This relation between the play and the main plot of *The Crying of Lot 49* points out the literary pattern making that lies at this novel's center. One can most quickly get to this center by determining whether or not the Tristero exists. Oedipa's attempts to determine that drive forward the plot, clearly indicating that the Tristero is vital to the novel's meaning. The play furnishes the necessary clue, and the connections between it and the main plot show a reader that to understand the Tristero one must first understand the play. In *The Courier's Tragedy* the Tristero's existence or non-existence hinges on a textual problem. Phrased more significantly, its status depends on whether or not the author, Wharfinger, actually mentions the Tristero in the play. By a fruitful analogy, the same point holds for Pynchon. Pynchon's relation to the Tristero matters most; Oedipa's relation to it matters less. That is, what Oedipa discovers about the Tristero matters less than the meanings Pynchon conveys by means of the Tristero. Understanding the enigma of the Tristero would soothe Oedipa, but it would end the novel. Most significant, Pynchon has made the question of the Tristero's existence the novel's basis, as he shows by declining to answer it at the end. Like the play in its relation to the main plot, the literary entity—in this case Pynchon's pattern making—dominates the nonliterary entity (Oedipa's attempts to understand the Tristero). The play, therefore, relates to the main plot as Pynchon's imagination relates to the novel.

To summarize this fairly abstruse and crucial point, by manipulating levels of reality—the play and the main plot— Pynchon shows how his book can be understood. Because the play explains the main action, one should look for an even more important literary entity that will explain the whole novel. All the lesser patterns converge to form one large pattern that the author constructs. Thus, at the simplest level Oedipa creates patterns. Here paranoia is an issue, because this malady perhaps causes her to understand things as she does. At the next level patterns develop between art and "reality." Paranoia does not matter here except as a metaphor for pattern making. At the highest level lie Pynchon's patterns, the dominant force in the novel. Here reference to paranoia does not solve any problems; in fact, its metaphoric meaning obscures far more than it clarifies. Pynchon again moves from raw data to a nonliterary way of organizing it to a literary way of organizing it, at first using the elements of fiction—here expecially plot and character—to frustrate common sense approaches.

In Dnubietna's poem in *V.* Pynchon lets his mask slip further, although this passage is far from straightforward:

> If I told the truth
> You would not believe me.
> If I said: no fellow soul
> Drops death from the air, no conscious plot
> Drove us underground, you would laugh
> As if I had twitched the wax mouth
> Of my tragic mask into a smile—
> A smile to you; to me the truth behind
> The catenary: locus of the transcendental:
> $y = a/2 (e^{x/a} + e^{-x/a})$ (pp. 305–306).

Again a work within a work furnishes a valuable clue to the meaning of the larger work. In the first seven lines Dnubietna, claiming that no plot exists, rejects a paranoid explanation of the German bombing of Malta during World War II. For it he substitutes a scientific explanation: that the bombing manifests the mathematical equation for the catenary, the curve formed by securing at two places a rope of uniform thickness and the route that a falling bomb will take. This substitution, however, does not end the matter. Before he quotes this poem Dnubietna explains that a poet must lie, meaning that he must not deny the paranoid's explanation; in the poem he speculates on the possibility of making such a denial. Because his poem discusses the validity of fictions, however, it implies more than it states explicitly. He has "lied" in a sense he does not fully grasp: he does not say that he has written a poem. One other level exists, because Pynchon has actually written the poem and worked it into his novel. Including Dnubietna's poem helps Pynchon develop this character, complicates the point of view by differentiating him from Pynchon, enriches the theme of creativity, and develops the setting by showing another way to understand Malta.

The apparent opposite of paranoia, which Pynchon calls anti-paranoia, offers little comfort. He develops most fully in *Gravity's Rainbow* this belief that nothing connects with anything else, so that no one can validly organize information, which terrifies the characters who believe it. At first some of them broach the idea by expressing skepticism about the possibility of control, which sounds less frightening than other ways to express it (p. 30). Later, characters conceive it as a lack of relationships: "anti-paranoia, where nothing is connected to anything" (p. 434). By the end of the novel, some of the characters think of anti-paranoia as a possibility equal to and opposite of paranoia, the two together forming an unacceptable yet inescapable dichotomy.

In Pynchon's first novel the roots of his conception of anti-paranoia can be discovered. He published a short story, "Under the Rose," that appears, extensively modified, in *V.* Some of the additions made for the novel are hints that things do not connect. In "Under the Rose" Moldwoerp, a German spy, opposes two British spies, Porpentine and Goodfellow, who begin to think that "Lepsius, Bongo-Shaftsbury, all the others, had been more than merely tools or physical extensions of Moldwoerp. They were all in it; all had a stake, acted as a unit. Under orders. Whose orders?" (p. 248). At the end of the story one learns that Goodfellow will be at Sarajevo in order to resist the plot to kill Archduke Ferdinand. To these two British spies, order thus becomes increasingly evident until it induces paranoid obsessions with plots. Besides changing to multiple points of view when he tells the story in *V.*, Pynchon revises it so as to break down connections (pp. 52–82). The episode in *V.* ends by implicitly blaming the difficulties experienced by the characters on the ambiguities of perception:

> Vision must be the last to go. There must also be a nearly imperceptible line between an eye that reflects and an eye that receives.
>
> The half-crouched body collapses. The face and its masses of white skin loom ever closer. At rest the body is assumed exactly into the space of this vantage. (p. 82)

Like the rest of this episode, the conclusion shows that evil exists, but it does not clarify its nature or establish its purposiveness.

Oedipa Maas, too, faces the possibility that nothing connects. Although it would be comforting for her to learn that Inverarity has not made the connections she thinks she has found, this would mean that she can have no easy alternative to San Narciso's banalities. In this novel anti-paranoia remains in the background, and the dominant dichotomy is paranoia and not-paranoia. Thus, although the characters in the first two novels have great difficulties, Pynchon's slight emphasis on anti-paranoia makes them seem less constricted than the characters in *Gravity's Rainbow*, who cannot find a third alternative and therefore believe that they must choose between paranoia and anti-paranoia.

As he develops the dichotomy of paranoia and anti-paranoia, Pynchon shows either that he thoroughly understands the German films of the period between the wars or that he understands the German culture and psychology of that period as thoroughly as did those filmmakers. In *From Caligari to Hitler* Siegfried Kracauer points out the suggestion frequently made by those films that the only political alternatives are tyranny and anarchy, the political analogues of paranoia and anti-paranoia.

For this reason Pynchon may have waited until he wrote his book that examines German sensibility before beginning to emphasize anti-paranoia. This political hypothesis causes many Germans to become increasingly desperate and thus helped create the situation that Hitler exploited. In a sense, Hitler resolved the dilemma by creating a tyranny while making political decisions, such as instituting his racial policy, that allowed free play to the most base of anarchic impulses.

Pynchon often relates aggression to paranoia. For example, in "Mortality and Mercy in Vienna" the Ojibwas' paranoia turns into aggression. Writing about *The Crying of Lot 49*, Richard Poirier makes a generalization that holds also for Pynchon's other novels: "In international relations the ecstasy is war; in human relationships it can be sado-masochism."[1] Pynchon's work contains so many descriptions of aggression that its existence requires no proof. Some of this aggression results from the inability of various characters to organize experience, and some results from ineffective means of organization, such as paranoia. Occasionally, as Poirier writes, aggression provides temporary release from the obligation to understand. Usually, however, its causes are not epistemological but social or psychological.

Another psychological trait to which Pynchon often refers, anality, does need illustration and explanation. Anal images abound in his novels. One of them, the sewers in *V.*, makes sense also as a symbol of the unconscious and as part of the motif of the underground. In his descriptions of the sewers Pynchon includes details that relate to his excremental theme. For example, Profane upon waking up in a bar realizes that the Puerto Ricans who work with him in the sewers "were carrying him down Amsterdam Avenue like pallbearers, all chanting, 'Mierda. Mierda. Mierda' " (p. 122). Shortly after that, Pynchon announces that "Angel and Geronimo had tried to smuggle parts of a toilet under their coats out of the men's room in a bar on Second Avenue" (p. 123).

In *Gravity's Rainbow* toilets, not sewers, relate to the theme of anality. In addition to Slothrop's trip into the plumbing to retrieve his harmonica, the behaviorist Pointsman during his first appearance in the novel puts his foot into a discarded toilet bowl and cannot pull it out. This scene hints at his anal-erotic personality. Pynchon's invention of a German toilet-ship and a rocket landing as Slothrop sits on the privy at the very beginning of the novel are further instances of the anal imagery. The narrator suggests one explanation, which he attributes to the Slothrops, for this image's frequency when he speaks about "shit, money, and the Word, the three American truths" (p. 28). In this novel, however, Pynchon includes little social criticism to support this thesis.

The other main psychological phenomenon in Pynchon's work, love, intertwines with sex and the cultural and social forces that oppose both. To begin with the negative, early in *Gravity's Rainbow* he quotes a statement on these matters: " 'I know there is wilde love and joy enough in the world,' preached Thomas Hooker, 'as there are wilde Thyme, and other herbes; but we would have garden love, and garden joy, of Gods owne planting' " (p. 22). Reasonable as this position may sound, it calls to mind the stereotyped conception of the Puritan sexual ethic. Other Puritans transformed Hooker's call for restraint into justification for stifling sexuality. Slothrop grew up in the Connecticut Valley upstream from Hartford, which Hooker and his congregation founded. Moreover, the Great Awakening began in this same valley, which was for decades a seedbed of Puritan thought. This geographical connection underscores the fact that Slothrop, and many other characters, must contend with Puritan ideology. Quantitatively, his sexual life is far from disappointing, if the map of his conquests can be believed, but there is little or no evidence that it is qualitatively satisfying. Capitalistic ideology also vitiates the erotic lives of these characters. Pynchon does not pursue this topic at much length, although a minor character in *Gravity's Rainbow* does say, " 'Look at the forms of capitalist expression. Pornographies: pornographies of love, erotic love, Christian love, boy-and-his-dog' " (p. 155). Inverarity's conglomerate in *The Crying of Lot 49* and the interlocking cartels in *Gravity's Rainbow* sufficiently document the capitalists' power. Pynchon does not indicate, however, that this power causes sexual repression. As if these ideological pressures were not enough impediment to love, the characters sometimes organize their own anti-love groups. An executive tells

Oedipa, " 'My big mistake was love. From this day I swear to stay off of love: hetero, homo, bi, dog or cat, car, every kind there is. I will found a society of isolates, dedicated to this purpose' " (p. 85). Oedipa had also recently heard of Inamorati Anonymous, an organization based on Alcoholics Anonymous that helps anyone in danger of falling in love.

Much more effectively than these groups, the widespread notion that people are inanimate makes love difficult and sexual exploitation easy. The other side of this coin, sexualizing nonhuman objects, has the same effects. *Gravity's Rainbow* contains many examples of that phenomenon, some of them very imaginative. A scientific example concerns Kryptosam, a chemical invented by Laszlo Jamf, who thus strikes another blow for the forces of evil. An advertising brochure announces that it "in the presence of some component of the seminal fluid . . . promotes conversion of the tyrosine into melanin, or skin pigment" (p. 71). This brings to mind the character who can change his color by changing the amount of melanin in his skin and also satirizes the popular misconception about the greater sexuality of dark-skinned people. Some of the narrator's speculations also eroticize the rocket. In a comic vein, characters in a bar sing a series of bawdy limericks about "different ways of Doing It with the A4 or its related hardware" (p. 306). For example:

> There was a young fellow named Hector,
> Who was fond of a launcher-erector.
> But the squishes and pops
> Of acute pressure drops
> Wrecked Hector's hydraulic connector. (p. 306)

Pynchon even writes an eroticized version of Hansel and Gretel in which Katje, Gottfried, and Captain Blicero consciously reenact the story as they perform elaborate sexual acts (p. 96 ff.).

These and other difficulties take their toll on the amatory lives of the characters. From his earliest works onward Pynchon has created characters driven to sexual excess, trying variation after variation and partner after partner in hopes of finding satisfaction. His first sexually frenzied character, Debby Considine, appears in his first story, "Mortality and Mercy in Vienna." Immediately after opening a conversation with Siegel, "she began reeling off a list of the affairs she had had in all the undeveloped areas she had visited for the State Dept.; several pages of unofficial statistics which sounded a little like the Catalogue aria from *Don Giovanni*" (p. 207). She is a prototype for the Whole Sick Crew of *V.*, for Metzger in *The Crying of Lot 49*, and for many characters in *Gravity's Rainbow*.

For other characters love is successfully consummated only at death. This Liebestod motif adds a poignant note to the love described in these novels. Although the clearest examples occur in Pynchon's first two books, this motif is more appropriate to *Gravity's Rainbow*, because the Germans have responded most strongly to Liebestod, as their mythology testifies. The narrator of *V.* alludes to this mythology as he indicates an example of this form of love: "As for V., she recognized—perhaps aware of her own progression toward inanimateness—the fetish of Mélanie and the fetish of herself to be one. As all inanimate objects, to one victimized by them, are alike. It was a variation on the Porpentine theme, the Tristan-and-Iseult theme, indeed, according to some, the single melody, banal and exasperating, of all Romanticism since the Middle Ages: 'the act of love and the act of death are one' " (p. 385). This conception of love, although it may ennoble the participants by raising them to a tragic level, also contains the seeds of their destruction, perhaps of their self-destruction.

One episode in *V.* ends with a comment that relates it to Liebestod:

A portable radio hung by his steering wheel, tuned to WQXR. Tchaikovsky's Romeo and Juliet Overture flowed syrupy around him and his passengers. As the bus crossed Columbus Avenue, a faceless delinquent heaved a rock at it. Cries in Spanish ascended to it out of the darkness. A report which could have been either a backfire or a gunshot sounded a few blocks downtown. . . . the eternal drama of love and death continued to unfold. (p. 83)

Here Liebestod, although not named, explains the yoking of two unlike phenomena: violence and Tchaikovsky's love music.

In his two most recent novels Pynchon handles this theme very differently. In *The Crying of Lot 49* the union of love and death is sick and criminal. The love becomes perverted, and thus the death, rather than becoming noble because it consummates love, remains merely death. Oedipa, already beginning to despair, sees "an advertisement by AC-DC, standing for Alameda County Death Cult. . . . Once a month they were to choose some victim from among the innocent, the virtuous, the socially integrated and well-adjusted, using him sexually, then sacrificing him" (p. 90). The narrator rejects this group with a terse understatement: "Oedipa did not copy the number" (p. 90). References to Wagner's operas, the primary musical expression of Liebestod, abound in *Gravity's Rainbow*. In fact, death pervades *Gravity's Rainbow*, so even the love that does not form a Liebestod exists against its backdrop.

Some of his characters turn to sexual variations, such as homosexuality, which occurs mainly in *Gravity's Rainbow* as bisexuality. For example, Pynchon, with some historical justification, sketches in a homosexual side to Blicero, the archetypal Nazi. According to George L. Mosse, Hans Blüher, a leading Nazi ideologist, thought that homosexuality allows diversion of emotional attachment and energy to cosmic concerns and to the Bund, a male elite organization.[2] The Nazis enlisted persons who had cosmic concerns by demonstrating to them the brand of pseudomysticism in their politics, and they used the Bunds as cadres. Thus, Pynchon here analyzes more than love during war, he knows, or senses the point that Mosse makes.

In all three novels Pynchon describes other sexual variations, the minority tastes already mentioned. Also, in *V.* Weissmann, who will become Captain Blicero in *Gravity's Rainbow*, briefly turns transvestite (p. 242). But another, misnamed, type of love, Heroic Love, interests Pynchon more. Mafia Winsome, a devotee of it, torments her husband, who has more ordinary erotic tastes. His down-to-earth description of Heroic Love in *V.* comes closer to the truth than does Mafia's mistakenly idealistic conception. " 'You are turning our marriage,' " he tells her, " 'into a trampoline act' " (p. 113). The narrator echoes this evaluation: "In practice Heroic Love meant screwing five or six times a night, every night, with a great many athletic, half-sadistic wrestling holds thrown in" (p. 113). The name of Oedipa's hometown, San Narciso, identifies the most important kind of unusual love in *The Crying of Lot 49*. Metzger, the ex-child star desperately trying to convince himself that he has retained his youth and attractiveness, is the leading practitioner but not the only one. Sadomasochism, which Pynchon depicts as the most disturbing corruption of love, holds the stage in *Gravity's Rainbow*. One character even argues, unconvincingly, that it can subvert an unjust social system: "Why will the Structure allow every other kind of sexual behavior but *that* one? Because submission and dominance are resources it needs for its very survival. They cannot be wasted in private sex" (p. 737). Joseph W. Slade articulates the reasoning of some of Pynchon's characters: "Sexual perversions are a reaction against the belief that life is determined" (*Thomas Pynchon*, p. 232).

Even though sadomasochism cannot overthrow societies, simpler forms of love can resist paranoia. At least, Evan Godolphin and Victoria Wrenn of *V.* find this to be true. Once, together, "at least they seemed to give up external plans, theories and codes, even the inescapable romantic curiosity about one another, to indulge in being simply and purely young" (p. 185). Many of Pynchon's characters discover that this kind of love can withstand not only paranoia but also other debilitating forces. After he creates nearly endless difficulties for his characters and shows them ensnarled in their much too intricate ways of escaping these difficulties, Pynchon indicates that the simple and long-recognized solution of love will work. He avoids sentimentality by describing the difficulties and other possible solutions first, rather than immediately presenting love as an ideal and then creating minor, accidental difficulties for the lovers.

Throughout his career Pynchon has presented complex intellectual problems and their simple emotional solution. The difficulties, overwhelming and pervasive, do not go away, but lovers create a space where the problems cannot reach them. Even in the early *Saturday Evening Post* story, "The Secret Integration," he describes young boys who have found this solution. Precocious in their insight into the adults' weaknesses, these boys discover the proper response to them. Their understanding does not become conscious, but they sense that "something inert and invisible, something they could not be cruel to or betray (though who would have gone so far as to call it love?) would always be between them and any clear or irreversible step" (p. 50).

Some characters are conscious of this thing, which definitely should be called love. In *V.* both Paola Maijstral and Rachel Owlglass, who have a substantial capacity for love, contrast dramatically with the characters whose motivations have become so entangled that they steadily move away from solutions. Paola, because she withstands both the effects of the war that raged during her youth and the vagaries of Benny Profane, offers a particularly attractive alternative to the Whole Sick Crew and their ilk. In *The Performing Self* Richard Poirier trenchantly describes the contrast in Pynchon's first two books between characters such as Rachel and Paola and the others: "Except for the heroine of *V.*, Rachel Owlglass, and the heroine of *The Crying of Lot 49*, Oedipa Maas—lovable, hapless, decent, eager girls—both novels are populated by self-mystified people running as if on command from the responsibilities of love to the fascination of puzzles and the power of things. No plot, political, novelistic, or personal, can issue from the circumstances of love, from the simple human needs . . . and Pynchon implicitly mocks this situation by the Byzantine complications of the plot."[3]

Jessica Swanlake in *Gravity's Rainbow* resembles Rachel, Paola, and Oedipa. To overcome the war she and Roger Mexico use the same method as do the three other women: "If they have not quite seceded from war's state, at least they've found the beginnings of gentle withdrawal . . . both know, clearly, it's better together, snuggled in, than back out in the paper, fires, Khaki, steel of the Home Front" (p. 41). These two characters, who appear occasionally throughout this novel, contrast with both the war and the substitutes for love. Pynchon, however, here turns out to be less sanguine about love's efficacy, at least as illustrated by these two characters. Near the end of the book Jessica realizes that " 'The War' was the condition she needed for being with Roger. 'Peace' allows her to leave him" (p. 628).

In contrast, after he realizes the efficacy of love Pökler, the tragic German engineer, remains steadfast. In addition to loving his daughter, he makes toward another person a gesture that, like

Oedipa's gesture toward the drunk, is actually directed to humanity. Near the Mittelwerke, "where it was darkest and smelled the worst, Pökler found a woman lying, a random woman. He sat for half an hour holding her bone hand. She was breathing. Before he left, he took off his gold wedding ring and put it on the woman's thin finger, curling her hand to keep it from sliding off. If she lived, the ring would be good for a few meals, or a blanket, or a night indoors, or a ride home. . . ." (p. 433). Here Pynchon shows that he has come a long way since *V.* He does not gratuitously present a comment such as "keep cool, but care" that will seem neither serious nor justified by the rest of the novel. Rather, he adopts a clear and appropriate tone, and with his erudition and control of tone throughout this book he earns the right to make such a simple plea. Pökler's action fits Pynchon's characterization of him, whereas McClintic Sphere in *V.* speaks with no authority. It is also important that Pökler silently acts, whereas Sphere only talks.

In his work, Pynchon alludes to some of the great builders of psychological systems. For example, Freud's theories about paranoia explain many details in Pynchon's work. Writing in *Totem and Taboo* on this subject, Freud states an idea closely resembling Pynchon's ideas about organizing information: "It might be maintained . . . that a paranoic delusion is a caricature of a philosophical system."[4] Far from denigrating philosophy, Freud here refers to the vast range of mankind's efforts to order information. Paranoia, like philosophical systems but much less competently, performs this task. Pynchon conceives of paranoia similarly, as an effort to make patterns, although unlike Freud he hesitates to condemn the paranoid.

In his examination of paranoia Freud often concentrates on its relation to meaning. Paranoids, he writes in *The Psychopathology of Everyday Life*, "attach the greatest significance to the minor details of other people's behaviour which we ordinarily neglect, interpret them and make them the basis of far-reaching conclusions."[5] He goes on to explain that paranoids, far from being baffled by the world, as other neurotics and psychotics are, find more meaning in it than do average people. Of the paranoid Freud says, "everything he observes in other people is full of significance, everything can be interpreted" (p. 255). Paranoids, thus, are the hermeneutics specialists among the emotionally disturbed, to whom the world is a huge text so obscure that it needs explanation. Furthermore, paranoids draw much more effectively than most people on the storehouse— whether it be a treasure house or charnel house—of the unconscious and transfer more material from it to the conscious mind. Because of these tendencies paranoids may seem to be geniuses who understand the world much better than most people do, but of course their perceptions obfuscate much more than they clarify. They misunderstand because they displace onto others what they dredge up from their own unconsciouses. Later psychologists sometimes dispute Freud's emphasis on this displacement, but his notion of the paranoid as a maker of unhelpful patterns accurately describes Pynchon's characters who have this neurosis.

Paranoia, according to Freud, also makes it difficult for people to achieve mature sexual love. He makes this claim in his most extensive case study of paranoia, "Analysis of a Case of Chronic Paranoia," in which he argues that this malady is caused by repression. Specifically, "what has been repressed is a sexual experience in childhood."[6] A person represses such an experience because he or she distrusts others, which causes projection (attributing to others qualities that one has repressed), a symptom of paranoia. An analyst has difficulty identifying the repressed material because "an analogous modern image takes the place of the repressed one" (p. 184). Reversing this psychological process—that is, overcoming repression by manifesting love and sexuality—one can conclude, will perhaps cure paranoia. Many of Pynchon's characters, although they do not articulate Freudian theories, sense the possibility of this cure. Conversely, many characters exhibit symptoms of both paranoia and repression or perversion of love, the two problems reinforcing each other until their psychological condition becomes hopeless.

Pynchon seems to have been influenced by two later psychologists who expanded on Freud's theories about anality, which Freud believes is the second of three stages of sexual development. Pynchon is likely to have used ideas from Erik

Erikson's *Young Man Luther*, a book that helps to explain modern Germany.[7] Erikson himself points out similarities between Hitler and Luther, such as their anal-eroticism (pp. 105–9). He and Pynchon describe many of the same details about wartime Germans. Although Pynchon does not mention it, a geographical coincidence links Luther and a setting that is important both to the history of Nazism and to *Gravity's Rainbow*. Nordhausen, the location of the Mittelwerke, lies only forty miles from Erfurt, where Luther obtained his university and monastic training, and only thirty miles from Eisleben, his birthplace. Anyone inclined to try the questionable task of sketching national characters in psychological terms can use the similarities between Hitler and Luther to attribute to Germans a tendency towards anality and can even go further to claim that widespread fixation in this sexual stage among Germans was a cause of Nazism's success.

Erikson argues that anality, like aggression, relates to paranoia, another relation that would interest anyone looking for the psychological causes of Nazism. Luther's obscenity, writes Erikson, "expresses the needs of a manic-depressive nature which has to maintain a state of unrelenting paranoid repudiation of an appointed enemy on the outside in order to avoid victimizing and, as it were, eliminating himself" (p. 246). Erikson goes on to describe Luther's paranoid focus on single figures such as the Pope and the Devil (p. 247). Pynchon creates characters with intense, carefully delimited paranoia like that which Erikson attributes to Luther. For example, many characters in *Gravity's Rainbow* focus their fear on the rocket.

Anality, Erikson also mentions, relates to magic, a frequently recurring motif in *Gravity's Rainbow*. As Erikson points out, Freud believed in this relation, too (*Young Man Luther*, p. 246). The connection goes back at least as far as an old folk tradition that "the devil and his home, and feces and the recesses of their origin, are all associated in a common underground of magic danger" (p. 62). Erickson claims that Luther, motivated by anal tendencies engendered by events in his early life, seized upon and sharpened this tradition. For example, Erikson claims that "in Luther's more popular imagery, the behind is the devil's magic face" (p. 122). Luther's tapping of this powerful psychological complex increased the effectiveness of his preaching and writing.

The other probable influence on Pynchon's treatment of anality, Norman O. Brown, expresses most of his insights on the subject in his classic essay on Swift.[8] Brown bases his analysis of anality on Freudian theory but diverges in his own direction. Beginning with the ideas in Freud's "Character and Anal Eroticism," Brown writes a critique of modern capitalism and science. Before he gets to the present era, he, too, invokes Luther and Swift. Like Erikson, he points out Luther's equation of the anal region and the devil. As evidence he recounts the story of Luther, while sitting on a privy, arriving at his belief in justification by faith. Pynchon demonstrates some knowledge of Brown's work when he refers in *Gravity's Rainbow* to polymorphous perversity, one of that psychologist's most important concepts (p. 440).

For his critique of capitalism Brown also borrows Freud's theory that people in the anal stage believe in a relationship between feces and property. As mentioned earlier, Luther related the demonic (and thus the magical) to the excremental. Brown then cites "Luther's vision of the demonic in capitalism" (p. 219), which adds a third member to the cluster, resulting in capitalism-demonism-excrement. Death joins this triumvirate when Brown charges that "the Protestant surrender to calling and to capitalism is a mode of surrender to the Devil and to death" (pp. 222–23). The reason for Brown's connection becomes more clear when he writes later that "life remains a war against death— civilized man, no more than archaic man, is not strong enough to die—and death is overcome by accumulating time-defying monuments" (p. 286). The death-magic-excrement part of this cluster occurs frequently in Pynchon's work, for example in the description of coal, lying deathlike and excremental underground waiting for "Kabbalists" to create synthetics from it.

According to Brown, technology also belongs to the cluster of negative entities. He points out the "connection between sublimation, the death instinct, and excrement" (p. 297), then he fixes blame: "technological progress makes increased sublimation possible" (p. 297). Pynchon's characters certainly fear technology, too, most intensely in *Gravity's Rainbow* because their fear focuses on the mordant rocket. Brown offers a way out of this predicament—satisfying our need for science and technology yet avoiding the damage they cause—by proposing a new kind of science. "What would a nonmorbid science look like?" he asks. "It would presumably be erotic rather than (anal) sadistic in aim" (p. 236). It is hard to imagine such a science literally, but Pynchon's characters try to preserve their erotic natures despite science's incursions into their lives. This effort accounts for some of their frenzied sexual excesses.

Lawrence C. Wolfley presents a more extensive account of Norman O. Brown's influence on *Gravity's Rainbow*. He claims, for example, that Brown is the major source for the theme of repression, which he believes is the major theme of that novel: "Gravity is the ultimate metaphor in the novel for the human repression that is its theme" (p. 876). He continues, "The primary locus for the theme of repression in *GR* is . . . Calvinism," which evinces an anal-erotic obsession with dominance in its insistence that the world is divided into the Elect and the Preterite. This psychological syndrome intensifies repression. Many characters in *Gravity's Rainbow* are repressed but, according to Wolfley, Pynchon suggests that there may be psychological healing: "The repressed, reified as Black tribesmen [the Hereros] return literally, back to that Europe which tried so hard to suppress the knowledge of their very existence" (p. 879). Wolfley comments on a theme that both Brown and Pynchon develop, the anal-erotic character of science, which is illustrated by Pointsman. Wolfley's long article also clarifies other details in *Gravity's Rainbow* through comparison to Brown's theories.

Among the psychologists besides Freud and the Freudians who influence Pynchon, Wolfgang Köhler plays an important but nearly invisible part. The scene at the beginning of *Gravity's Rainbow* after the opening description of the refugees resists full explanation, but it probably relies on Köhler's experiments with apes (*The Mentality of Apes*) and on Robert Yerkes's experiments with chimpanzees (*Chimpanzees: A Laboratory Colony*), as the omnipresent bananas and the characters' subhuman actions suggest. In general, Köhler's early work creates a context for the many instances when Pynchon's characters act like totally controlled laboratory animals. Köhler's later work, when he was the leading exponent of Gestalt psychology, forms more analogies with Pynchon's work. A lucid, succinct statement of this school's first principle appears in his *Gestalt Psychology*: "The organism responds to the *pattern* of stimuli to which it is exposed."[9] Pynchon's characterization, plot construction, and conception of literature accord with this statement. As the familiar pictorial illustrations of this school of psychology show, in perception the whole is often greater than the sum of the parts because people construct patterns to make sense of seemingly disconnected data. For example, one of the illustrations appears to change back and forth from a vase to two human profiles, depending on the pattern that the perceiver forms. Pynchon's characters and his readers experience similar changing perceptions.

Jungian psychology explains some of Pynchon's imagery, such as the round Herero villages, which can be likened to mandalas, the symbol that Jung claims represents the unified self. Pynchon bluntly draws this analogy: "The village [was] built like a mandala" (p. 321). Later Andreas, a Herero, sees two mandalas connected with the rocket's control switch and fins:

> Andreas sets [the controls] on the ground, turns it till the K points northwest. "Klar," touching each letter, "Entlüftung, these are the female letters. North letters. In our villages the women lived in huts on the northern half of the circle, the men on the south. The village itself was a mandala. Klar is fertilization and birth, Entlüftung is the breath, the soul. Zündung and Vorstufe are the male signs, the activities, fire and preparation or building. And in the center, here, Hauptstufe. It is the pen where we kept the sacred cattle. The souls of the ancestors. All the same here. Birth, soul, fire, building. Male and female, together.
>
> The four fins of the Rocket made a cross, another mandala. Number one pointed the way it would fly. Two for pitch, three for yaw and roll, four for pitch. Each opposite pair of vanes worked together, and moved in opposite senses. Opposites together." (p. 563)

Andreas resembles an orthodox Jungian analyst with very strange scientific ideas. Like the Jungians, for example, he emphasizes the union of opposites. Specifically, his reference to the union of male and female recalls Jung's notion that the male and female sides (animus and anima) of a personality must be reconciled.

Elsewhere in *Gravity's Rainbow* Pynchon extends this web of imagery by mentioning that the launching pad "is set inside a space defined by three trees, blazed so as to triangulate the exact bearing, 260°, to London." The rocket crew uses "a rude mandala, a red circle with a thick black cross inside, recognizable as the ancient sun-wheel from which tradition says the swastika was broken by the early Christians" (p. 100). This time the narrator draws a comparison, showing that Germans, like Hereros, responded strongly to the mandala, if one accepts the Jungian interpretation that their unconsciouses impelled them to select these figures. This example also is ironic, for Jung's positive symbol becomes part of a destructive device and turns into the Nazi insignia.

The mandala, along with other primordial images, exists, according to Jung, in the collective unconscious. The narrator of *V.* refers to this concept: "an ancestral memory, an inherited reservoir of primordial knowledge which shapes certain of our actions and casual desires" (p. 183). In *Gravity's Rainbow* Pynchon identifies the source of this idea: "So that the right material may find its way to the right dreamer, everyone, everything involved must be exactly in place in the pattern. It was nice of Jung to give us the idea of an ancestral pool" (p. 410). About *V.*, particularly its sewer images, Tony Tanner writes, "Hints at the possible existence of an inherited reservoir of primordial knowledge suggest that a deliberate Jungian dimension has been added. The notion that the unconscious nourishes art, even if the unconscious is comparable to a sort of primeval sewer, and that there is much to be gained by descending into our dreams, is so customary by now that one can see that Pynchon has gone some way to turning it into dark farce—Benny and the alligators" (*City of Words*, p. 166).

Pynchon, however, uses the concept of the collective unconscious productively as well as satirizing it. For example, the concept of the collective unconscious partially explains his theory of images. At the center of his first two books lie V. and the Tristero. These abstractions are somewhat vague; if they were images, they probably would be more comprehensible. Not coincidentally, in *Gravity's Rainbow* Pynchon first explicitly mentions Jung and uses his ideas extensively and then places at the center an image, the rocket, which provides a much sharper focus for this novel. He develops the image at length and adds an extensive emotional component to it, almost as if trying to create a Jungian archetype. The rocket finally connects to so many other images and ideas that it casts much light on the era of World War II.

Pavlov also figures prominently in *Gravity's Rainbow*. His famous work on conditioning permeates the characterization, although Pynchon rarely refers explicitly to it. Jamf has conditioned Slothrop psychologically; at least, Slothrop suspects this. A group of British psychologists led by the evil Pointsman carries out conditioning experiments, certainly on animals such as an octopus, and possibly on human subjects. Some of the characters think that someone or something they do not know has conditioned them. Pökler, for example, suspects that the Nazis are conditioning him in return for letting him see his daughter once a year. He always feels vaguely, and sometimes thinks clearly, that this arrangement alters his behavior to make him more valuable to the Nazis. The Nazis indeed do more than make an open agreement with him; they also manipulate him psychologically. More pathetically, many of the characters do not realize that conditioning has circumscribed their freedom of action.

Pavlov's reductivist notion that it is possible to find a physiological explanation for every human act plays an important part in *Gravity's Rainbow*. As his main disciple among the characters in this novel, Pointsman, says, Pavlov's "faith ultimately lay in a pure physiological basis for the life of the psyche" (p. 89). For example, one chapter of the book on Pavlovian psychology that Pointsman furtively shares with other devotees of Pavlov is entitled "An Attempt at a Physiological Interpretation of Obsessions and Paranoia." This "attempt" may sound encouraging: if paranoia and other psychological problems have only physiological causes, perhaps they can be cured simply, for example with medication. However, to give credence to such explanations is to adopt a very low view of human nature; the difficulty with doing that is not only the resulting theoretical mistakes but also the social corollaries such as the Puritans' notion of the Preterite and the harshest kinds of German colonial policy, which devastated the Hereros and others.

A less well-known aspect of Pavlov's system, his theory of opposites, also recurs in this novel, explaining the same dualistic phenomena as do cybernetics and the workings of the computer. Pointsman, "like his master I.P. Pavlov before him, . . . imagines the cortex of the brain as a mosaic of tiny on/off elements" (p. 55). Here again a distressingly materialistic idea equates man and machine and describes the human brain as a second-rate computer. Pavlov also applied his model of human thought to explain mental illness. According to the narrator of *Gravity's Rainbow* he (Pavlov) "thought that all the diseases of the mind could be explained, eventually, by the ultraparadoxical phase, the pathologically inert points on the cortex, the confusion of ideas of the opposite" (p. 90). Bizarre though this idea is, it fits well with the motif of opposites that pervades Pynchon's books, especially in relation to cybernetics.

Pavlov's theory of opposites explains two important themes in *Gravity's Rainbow*, one of which has been important throughout Pynchon's literary career. The enduring theme, reported by the narrator, is Pavlov's theory that faulty conceptions of opposites cause paranoia. He thought that if the centers in the cortex that deal with opposites are damaged, "you weaken this idea of the opposite, and here all at once is the paranoid patient who would be master, yet now feels himself a slave" (p. 48). If Pavlov is correct, Oedipa Maas's efforts to escape systems of opposites will backfire, thus provoking the very psychological problem that she wants to cure. Pavlovian psychology cannot explain as satisfactorily a second theme of *Gravity's Rainbow*: the rocket. To compose an explanation the Pavlovians in this novel consider two kinds of rocket, "V-1 and V-2, one the reverse of the other. . . . Pavlov showed how mirror-images Inside could be confused. Ideas of the opposite. But what new pathology lies Outside now? What sickness to events—to History itself—can create symmetrical opposites like these robot weapons?" (p. 144).

This analysis engenders little conviction, since the differences between these two rockets are trivial compared to other features of the rockets in this novel.

Two ways in which Pynchon develops all these psychological methods of organizing information reveal their inadequacy. First, he refers to several different methods, thereby suggesting that no single psychological system is adequate. Second, his development of the love theme indicates that psychological information can prevent people from finding more satisfactory ways of understanding the world. Some characters simply love. Others, too aware of the psychological implications of sex and love, cannot achieve either satisfactorily. Psychological information thus sometimes leads not to a better life but to a worse one.

4.

History

As he does with scientific and psychological information, Pynchon scatters bits of historical information throughout his short stories and novels. When he considers methods of organizing information, however, he probes more deeply into history than into the other two disciplines. That is, he alludes not to the ways that individual historians organize information but to ideas about the nature of history. This analysis of historiography shows the basic ways one can conceive of history's flow, which underlie individual compilations of history.

He refers to social and political history, although with less emphasis than some critics have claimed and usually in conjunction with an implicit moral dimension. One example of his social commentary, a description of the cruelty inflicted on the Maltese, appears in *V.* He sketches in a little of Maltese history, but perhaps less than is needed to indicate that the Maltese are a paradigmatic downtrodden people.[1] During their first few centuries of recorded history they lived more placidly than later. The Carthaginians colonized Malta in the eighth and seventh centuries B.C. In 218 B.C. Rome took over, the first of many changes of possession that make Malta seem like a coin changing hands in the marketplace of power politics. In the sixth century A.D. the Byzantines supplanted the Romans, and in 870 were in turn replaced by the Moslems. Thus, even in the Middle Ages it became clear that Malta had a strategic location—directly in the path of any state in the Mediterranean area that became a first-class power and felt obliged to expand. At the same time the topsoil of the island wore away, exacerbating the land's parched condition, which was caused by low rainfall. To the victors belonged few spoils, to the Maltese even fewer, but this did not deter prospective victors.

After this era conqueror followed conqueror at an even faster rate. In 1091 Roger the Norman assumed control, but his successors did not expel all the Moslems until the 1240s. By the fifteenth century all the soil had disappeared from the infertile limestone base and depopulation had made the country even poorer. And still the conquerors came. In 1530 Suleiman and the Turks drove the Knights of St. John out of Rhodes, and they chose Malta as their new residence. Thirty-five years later the Turks followed, laying the Great Siege, which ultimately failed. As long after that as the seventeenth century the Turks continued to menace the island, and pirates used it as a base, adding to the turmoil. In 1798 Napoleon joined the list of Malta's rulers: conquering it, moving on, and leaving behind a garrison. An uprising of the Maltese and a British blockade of the island also occurred during that year. The British drove out the French two years later and kept control for more than a century. In 1940, during an era that Pynchon describes in *V.*, the Italians bombed the island because it served as a base for Allied airplanes and submarines, and later they attacked unsuccessfully by sea. At the same time there was a food shortage. Finally, in 1964, Malta achieved the independence that it so clearly deserves.

The island of Malta, because of its composition, is a natural symbol of rocklike endurance. Moreover, the Maltese people's strength of character is symbolized by their environment's rock. Pynchon thus forms an analogy between history and geography in the case of Malta. Paola Maijstral and her father, after he matures, exhibit this strength. Malta's history also calls into question a psychological explanation of reality. That is, a fearful Maltese may be realistic rather than paranoid; his island's past offers ample evidence that hostile forces actually have tried to destroy his countrymen. In *V.* and *Gravity's Rainbow* Malta is a timeless symbol of man's inhumanity to man.

As another part of his dramatization of social and political history, Pynchon depicts the exploitation of minorities. A full understanding of the most important example in his work, his account of the Hereros, requires knowledge of facts that he does not mention.[2] Their habitat, Southwest Africa, has even fewer geographical attractions than Malta, except for the diamonds that lured some exploiters and did the natives little good. Its low rainfall—an average of 10.7 inches a year—makes it marginally acceptable for human existence. Improbably, Germany founded its first colony in this land. In 1882 Adolf Lüderitz obtained German protection for any part of the territory he acquired, and his agent, Heinrich Vogelsang, began to buy land. A Hedwig Vogelsang appears in *V.*; perhaps Pynchon intends her to be a relative of Heinrich. In 1884 Britain agreed to make the territory a German protectorate, and Bismark accordingly allowed Lüderitz to form a chartered company.

At this point the suffering of the Hereros, onerous when stronger countries left them alone, became more intense. When the chief of the Hereros died in 1891, the Germans sought to replace him with a puppet, thereby revealing the plans they had for the Hereros. Soon German traders began to exploit the natives, and Germans who came to settle began to expropriate the land and women. The Hereros suffered greatly during the Rinderpest (cattle plague) of 1897–98, because the Germans failed to inoculate the Hereros' cattle, which, in addition to providing the staple food, of sour milk, were their main source of wealth. In 1904 the Hereros rebelled, and von Trotha, whose grisly work Pynchon mentions in both *V.* and *Gravity's Rainbow*, arrived with orders to exterminate them. Natural forces prevailed even though von Trotha did not. Although the battle of Waterberg (or Hamakari) was indecisive in itself, thousands of Hereros died from thirst as they tried to flee its site. Von Trotha then stepped up his campaign, killing, according to Pynchon, sixty thousand. At this point even members of the Reichstag condemned the chartered company's policy. In 1915 an army from South Africa conquered the Germans, and the Union of South Africa received a mandate to govern under the auspices of the League of Nations. Far from a saving grace, this political change merely substituted one group of exploiters for another less direct one. The new rulers moved the Hereros inland into the almost uninhabitable Kalahari Desert, where they remain and where only one-fiftieth of their land can support cattle. This historical context both justifies and makes credible the Hereros' efforts in *Gravity's Rainbow* to obtain the Germans' rocket secrets.

Two short stories and one essay exhibit Pynchon's concern for other minorities. In "Mortality and Mercy in Vienna" the Ojibwa social structure and the larger society that dominates it share some of the blame for Irving Loon's paranoia. In "The Secret Integration" Pynchon shows the need for greater racial understanding. His use of small boys to make his point somewhat sentimentalizes it, and he emphasizes the boys' perception of their town rather than making an incisive social analysis. At about the same time, he wrote "Journey into the Mind of Watts," a study of that community nine months after the riots, in which he disagrees with the official view that the riots had awakened concern and that Watts's problems were being solved. He meticulously describes the reality of Watts to support his thesis that "the white culture is concerned with various forms of systematized folly—the economy of the area in fact depending on it—the black culture is stuck pretty much with basic realities like disease, like failure, violence and death, which the whites have mostly chosen—and can afford—to ignore" (p. 148). In general, Pynchon has demonstrated both understanding of and concern for the plight of minority groups, but in his novels he subordinates this concern to other matters. If he wanted to be polemical about minorities, he probably would have taken the opportunity afforded by the historical background of *Gravity's Rainbow* to describe the effects of Hitler's racial and ethnic policy. Instead, he rarely mentions Jewish suffering, writing instead about the little-known Hereros and their search for the rocket, which he invents, rather than their real suffering.

At its most specific, Pynchon's analysis of suffering deals with individuals. By obscuring the causes of this suffering he makes it appear ahistorical. For example, many characters, such as Oedipa

Maas, do not understand the reasons for their troubles, and Pynchon, far from identifying historical causes, makes this obscurity part of the point of his works. That is, as he sketches in epistemological puzzles he partially erases the historical dimension of his characters' difficulties. His social analysis consists almost entirely of describing problems rather than of laying out causes or suggesting cures. The problems then become aspects of nonsocial and nonhistorical topics, such as psychological difficulties, or they are subsumed into literary effects, like Malta's transformation from a scene of hardship into a symbolic setting.

Popular culture is a part of social history about which Pynchon writes. In *V.*, for example, he portrays characters watching a western on television, showing that their attraction to violence influences both their taste for westerns and their actions. Like his first two novels, *Gravity's Rainbow* contains allusions to popular culture, but it differs from the other books in that popular culture also shapes sections of its narrative. For example, the episode that recounts Tchitcherine's experiences in Central Asia is modeled on Western movies. The narrator explains that "in the mornings after mess, Tchitcherine will usually mosey down to the red dzurt there, fixing to look in on that Galina the schoolmarm" (p. 339). Pynchon thus integrates popular culture much more fully into this novel; he refers to it more often and examines more different types of it than in his earlier novels. In this novel comic strips work the same way as do popular films. For example, the episodes describing Rocketman and Plechazunga (the pig hero), especially in their plots, use comic strip conventions.

Pynchon writes very little about political history. The Tristero and V., although they are plots, are not political. Even the characters who believe in their existence and who claim to understand some of their attributes do not view them as political but believe that the plots oppose them as individuals, with no political causes or effects. Occasionally a character or a narrator mentions economic causes of the war in *Gravity's Rainbow*, but most often the war merely persists, inescapable yet inexplicable. This is not to say, of course, that Pynchon regards the war as nonpolitical. Its political background is well known; Pynchon attends to other things. For all these reasons historical events in his novels rarely seem to have political causes. In fact, sometimes politics are described abstractly, even metaphorically, as in a comment in *V.*: "Right and Left; the hothouse and the street. The Right can only live and work hermetically, in the hothouse of the past, while outside the Left prosecute their affairs in the streets by manipulated mob violence" (p. 440).

Although Pynchon does not often refer to social and political history, his works are full of references to the history of science and the history of communications. For example, a very brief history of rocketry through World War II will clarify many details in *Gravity's Rainbow*.[3] Early work by a Russian, Tsiolkovsky, lay for a long time in fallow ground. Finally, Robert H. Goddard, an American who is known as the father of modern rocketry, made the next important advances. His tests began, probably not coincidentally, in the war year of 1915 and lasted until 1941 under his own auspices, and under the military's from then until his death in 1945. A leading rocket scientist, and more important, a publicist for rocketry, Hermann Oberth, was born in 1894 in Transylvania, now part of Hungary but at that time under Germany's control. His books *The Rocket into Planetary Space* (1923) and *The Road to Space Travel* (1929) did much to augment public interest in rocket research. In 1931 at Dessau he and others launched the first liquid-propellant rocket; later they moved to an abandoned dump near Berlin. In 1932 the leading figure of German rocketry during World War II, Wernher Von Braun, went to work for the army. Five years later German rocket research moved to Peenemünde, a secluded location on the Baltic. On the Allied side just prior to the war Duncan Sandys, Churchill's son-in-law, led a British experimental rocket team. Pynchon refers to many of these scientists in his novel. The Germans of course progressed much more rapidly than any other group and they fired more than four thousand V-2 rockets at Britain during 1944 and 1945. It is these rockets that the British in *Gravity's Rainbow* try to counter. After the British air raid on Peenemünde on August 17, 1943, the Germans moved their operations to the Mittelwerke near Nordhausen in the Harz Mountains, where some of the action of *Gravity's Rainbow* occurs.

At the outbreak of war Allied spy networks inevitably turned much of their attention to discovering information about German scientific work, and they substantially increased their efforts when the rockets began to land. In Britain, Duncan Sandys, who appears in this novel, halted his own experiments and began trying to discover Germany's secrets. British intelligence obtained a scientific liaison, Dr. R. V. Jones, who became chief of the Scientific Intelligence Branch of the Air Ministry, and in December, 1943, began a coordinated effort called Operation Crossbow. Dr. A. D. Crow, Lord Cherwell, and Sir Stafford Cripps (the minister of Aircraft Production) also played prominent roles in this endeavor. In July, 1944, the Polish underground delivered to the British a German missile and a Polish engineer to help them study it, a coup that resulted in Project Big Ben, led by Crow, which tried to learn the missile's secrets. This group believed that the Germans would not find a suitable catalyst and that their program would thus fail. This underestimation reveals how little they knew about the Germans' Rocket Program: the first rockets struck England on August 8, 1944. These intelligence efforts, turned into fictional form, comprise the skeleton of *Gravity's Rainbow*. Beneath the glossy skin of the style and the twisted sinews of the plot, this structure creates order and stability for the novel.

At first the American equivalent of these British scientific intelligence operations was called Overcast; later the name was changed to Paperclip. Its most important participants included Gervais Trichel (chief, Rocket Branch, Army Ordinance), Holger Toftoy (chief of Ordinance Technical Intelligence), Robert Staver (in charge of research rocket installations and technicians), Richard Porter (the head of General Electric's Project Hermes, who worked under Staver), and James Hamill (in charge of evaluating rockets). From the information on these men in the standard histories of the American and British efforts, it is clear that none of them served as the model for Slothrop.

Immediately after the war, during the period described in *Gravity's Rainbow*, the intensity of intelligence efforts increased enormously. Pynchon's account of the time, as Friedman and Puetz demonstrate, is remarkably accurate (p. 355). Searchers were able to find much material in addition to the successful rockets and the few duds that the underground had previously recovered behind German lines at great risk. Nearly all the important

German scientists had escaped the German authorities and were open to blandishments. The German Rocket Technology was not to remain secret for long because the Mittelwerke and its rockets remained intact, and German scientists had moved voluminous files from Peenemünde to the Harz region near the Mittelwerke. Pynchon's novelistic version of a search for a new German rocket also has some basis in historical fact, since at the end of the war the Germans had a series of rockets in various stages of development from planning to testing. They had tested the A-4B, a V-2 with changes designed to increase its range, and they were planning five others, the most formidable of which was the A-10, a two-stage rocket with a 2,500-mile range. The Americans, by refusing to honor commitments to their Allies, won the biggest prizes. The Mittelwerke lay in the region that the allies had awarded to Russia, and the Americans had agreed previously to ship half of the rockets they found to Britain. Americans, however, roamed freely through the Harz region and sent all available rockets back to their own country. Staver found and removed a cache of valuable scientific documents from an area just before it was due to revert to Britain. The Russians meanwhile managed to induce a few scientists to join them. Staver received a report, probably false, that a Russian major was in charge of the facilities that once belonged to Germany and that he was making rockets. Perhaps it was this report that stimulated Pynchon to invent Tchitcherine.

The information from the history of communication that Pynchon uses concerns postal systems and forms part of the background of *The Crying of Lot 49*. Critics have explained most of the Tristero's meaning but not all of its basis in historical fact. For example, Anne Mangel, in her useful article, fails to recognize alternate names of the family that controlled the largest system in Europe, simply because she does not know one particular fact about the history of postal services. In his invented historical background for the Tristero, Pynchon mentions only a few facts about the Thurn and Taxis system, which really was for many centuries the official postal system in much of Europe. For example, he correctly says that "Taxis" may have derived from the Italian word *tasso*, "badger," and he mentions the emblem of the Messengers' guild (the post horn) and the badger and post horn on the family's coat of arms. But one needs to understand more about this system in order to understand the Tristero.

The Tristero began in Venice in 1305 as the Company of Couriers of the Most Illustrious Signoria. [4] These couriers tied a badger skin over the forehead of their horses; the plural of *tasso* (*tassi*) became first a family name and then the name of the system. By 1490 the family had expanded its operations as far as Innsbruck. In 1512 Maximilian ennobled Baptista Tassi and changed the family name to von Taxis. About the same time another member of the family was postmaster in Vienna, and in 1505 Franz Taxis built one postal route for King Philip from Spain to the Netherlands and another to Innsbruck so that the king could communicate with Maximilian. He later extended the Innsbruck route to Rome, so that by early in the Renaissance the family's couriers traveled almost from one end of Europe to the other. As the family dispersed, some of its branches took slightly different names that were appropriate to the countries in which they lived. In 1650, through a falsification of genealogies, the family proclaimed themselves the house of Torre e Taxis. Some of the German offshoots called themselves von Thurn und Taxis, and in 1844 the Prince de la Tour et Taxis signed a postal treaty with the king of France. Manfred Puetz has helpfully explained the historical context in which this system operated, as well as the degree of Pynchon's historical accuracy.[5]

This family did not build such a vast empire without opposition. Postal routes were very profitable, and their owners were able to establish close ties to noble and royal families, who, because of the high cost of the service, were almost the only customers. Later, as mentioned, the family itself became nobles. In many places and at many times the Thurn and Taxis family struggled to maintain their advantages against rival systems and eventually began to lose, and so it is apparent that alternate systems such as the Tristero do have historical basis. As the Holy Roman Empire waned so did the Thurn and Taxis, for when countries left the empire they established their own postal systems. The Congress of Vienna restored some areas to the Thurn and Taxis, but this measure did not reverse the ebbing tide. Finally, in 1867 the Prussian postmaster bought out the last Taxis manager. The long history and great power of the Thurn and Taxis and the ease with which it at first drove rivals out of business make it unlikely that an alternate system such as the Tristero could persist for centuries. Nevertheless, one of the dominant system's rivals may have secretly endured, lending credence to Oedipa's hopes for an alternative communication system and a concomitant way of life.

Since postal services control much information, they have great social implications. Money and power derive partly from information, particularly when communications are poor. A character in *The Crying of Lot 49* recognizes these connections and tries to show that the American postal reform movement of the 1840s and 1850s caused the Civil War (p. 35). His project seems less fanciful when one remembers that in the era before electronic communication a very high percentage of the information transmitted traveled by means of the postal system. Hence, it makes some sense to expect an alternate postal system to help overthrow the forces that dominate a society, partly by controlling the official postal system. Yearning for a better society, some of the characters want to believe that the Tristero exists. The Tristero, however, may already have been seized by Pierce Inverarity, a less than idealistic rebel whose aim is to take over large portions of the society and, rather than reform them, use them to his own advantage. On the other hand, he also may have acquired enough power to scatter clues about the Tristero in order to tantalize and frustrate dissidents.

In addition to these historical facts, Pynchon mentions several historiographical issues. R.W.B. Lewis almost identifies this most important aspect of Pynchon's use of history when he calls *V.* "a novel quite literally *about* history and possibly about the termination of history" (p. 228). He strays off course, however, when he becomes more specific: "The symbolism has to do with nothing less than the settled meaning of modern history" (p. 228). The word "settled" causes the misdirection, because history, like all other disciplines, is not, cannot be, settled. *V.*, like Pynchon's other two novels, is indeed about history, and about other intellectual disciplines, but it is also about the various ways in which these disciplines order data.

In *V.* Pynchon himself provides the necessary clue about his most important use of history. After mentioning two very different but simultaneous events, a cease-fire in the Mideast and the marriage of Grace Kelly and Prince Rainier, the narrator reports that "people read what news they wanted to and each accordingly built his own rathouse of history's rags and straws" (p. 209). The history of an era, then, does not exist; histories exist, perhaps one for each person who tries to understand the era. Some of Pynchon's characters reveal, either implicitly or explicitly, their methods of organizing historical facts, and his narrators, in their comments on the action, also sometimes show their own methods. And finally, Pynchon himself, by arranging his plots in distinctive ways, illustrates some methods.

Among the critics who have published studies of Pynchon, James D. Young, by commenting on Pynchon's fictions, his methods of organizing information, has most effectively used Pynchon's clues about history. As to historical fictions, Pynchon, according to Young, employs the principle that "if we can formulate an easy generalization to make order of the past, we can destroy the validity of that generalization by knowing more of the actual past" (p. 73). Here Young reveals part of the truth; Pynchon does present more information than any fiction can organize. However, he also shows that more than one method of organization works, even that more than one method works for a limited set of data. The welter of possible methods, even more than the welter of possible data, demonstrates history's fictiveness. By mixing "hard facts" with imaginative "facts," Pynchon, according to Young, proves that one cannot distinguish between the two and that therefore "one cannot separate history from fiction" (p. 74). But if one cannot separate history from fiction, it seems at least irrelevant and perhaps misleading to insist on the distinction. More logically, one should conclude that history is fictive because a person cannot understand the past without a means of organizing it. Generally, however, Young's article makes an important contribution, even though because of its brevity he cannot offer many examples or draw many conclusions.

One can best understand historians' ways of organizing data by first analyzing their premises about several fundamental issues, such as the existence and nature of time. To understand these issues one needs to begin with the most basic question: whether or not time exists. Partly because of his nationality, Fausto Maijstral feels compelled to deal with this issue: "But we are torn, our grand 'Generation of '37.' To be merely Maltese: endure almost mindless, without sense of time? Or to think—continuously—in English, to be too aware of war, of time . . . ?" (p. 289). This final alternative precludes historical understanding, but by denying the war along with other temporal events it makes for a more comfortable intellectual life. Finally, however, the war intrudes and Fausto has to admit that it and time exist. In *Gravity's Rainbow* the Hereros seek unsuccessfully to achieve timelessness: "What Enzian wants to create will have no history. It will never need a design change. Time, as time is known to the other nations, will wither away inside this new one" (pp. 318–19). Most of Pynchon's other characters either assume from the beginning that time exists or eventually arrive at this position. In any case, belief in timelessness never becomes a viable option.

If one assumes that time exists, one should next try to determine its nature. One such effort in *V.* has strange results. Fausto thinks of a conception of time that almost reinstates the theory of timelessness. In metaphorical terms he considers the possibility that time exists but remains static: "The room, though windowless and cold at night, is a hothouse. Because the room is the past, though it has no history of its own" (p. 285). If the room truly were a hothouse its heat would remain relatively constant in spite of the Second Law of Thermodynamics. That is, a hothouse, because it compensates for the heat lost at night, symbolizes time's resistance to change. Paradoxically, because it does not change, it has a past but no history. This theory would be attractive to a Maltese who is aware of the invader's virtually constant dominance of his country, during which nothing really changes.

The basis for another metaphor and for another theory of time and history lies just outside the window of Fausto's room. The street represents the more common linear conception of time and thus of the susceptibility to change of the past and present. A person walking down a street and thereby experiencing different things as he goes symbolizes mankind's progress through time and history. For example, the narrator imagines "the street of the 20th Century, at whose far end or turning—we hope—is some sense of home or safety" (p.303). The lure of better times possibly lying ahead makes this an attractive metaphor. Many Maltese during World War II, continually subjected to the horrors of war, would look to future relief and thereby would be tempted to view time as dynamic. Most of Pynchon's characters, especially those engaged in a quest, act as though they would accept this metaphor for history.

Theories of time likely will have corollaries about memory, and these, too, will have historiographical implications. Fausto complicates his meditation on time and history by announcing the chimerical nature of memory. To him, memory has no reality because it depends on an immutable identity (p. 287). That is, the rememberer must be identical with the person whose actions he remembers; otherwise the memory becomes distorted beyond recognition. Fausto does not have a consistent identity because dramatic changes in his personality divide his life into distinct periods; and he thus generalizes that memory has no validity for anyone. If he has reasoned correctly, time may exist but no one can accurately understand it, and thus history is real but also hopelessly jumbled. Fausto's line of reasoning, doubtful at best, is not confirmed by the rest of V. but it does help to characterize him.

If one believes that time and history do exist, one of his next concerns should be to determine the way in which history moves. He can do this by visualizing its movements as if they lay on a graph. Most of the historiography in Pynchon's books can be elucidated in this way. If history is nondetermined, a broken line will graph its movement. For example, Dnubietna in V. conceives of history as a step-function (p. 310). This curve, which looks like the horizontal component of a staircase, represents a discontinuous function. Such a conception would be attractive to a resident of Malta who knows that his island's history has been a series of unpredictable invasions and resulting periods of submission to foreign conquerors. Furthermore, Dnubietna, the engineer-poet, would naturally express this theory in mathematical terms.

One would graph the movements of history as a sequence of sine curves if he or she thinks that "her rhythms pulse regular and sinusoidal" (*V.*, p. 287). In the curve each half-cycle is a parabola, like the rocket's flight. This graph depicts history as a series of rising and falling periods that repeat the same movements but not the same content. According to this theory, civilizations lying at the same point on different curves resemble each other in the level of their development but differ in details. In this respect the sine-curve theory differs from the cyclical theory, which posits exact repetition. The progressions and declines of dominant civilizations usually determine the rises and falls.

Pynchon has ideas about two of the sine curve's segments as they explain historical actualities. The lowest point of each cycle manifests brutality and decadence. One such era, the Jacobean, plays a part in both *V.* and *The Crying of Lot 49*. The narrator of *V.* notes its position on history's curve: "In the next rising period of history, when this Decadence was past . . . , a dental historian would mention Eigenvalue in a footnote as . . . discreet physician to the neo-Jacobean school" (p. 277). Because of its reductiveness Eigenvalue's psychodontics is a measure of his decadence. The other deluded medical man in this novel, Schoenmaker the plastic surgeon, would also be at home in the Jacobean era. His treatment of Esther, both medically and sexually, amply demonstrates his brutality, and his sexual treatment of her also demonstrates his decadence. The narrator recognizes Schoenmaker's Jacobean attributes when he comments about his relation to Esther: "Such was the (as it were) Jacobean etiology of Esther's eventual trip to Cuba" (p. 98). In summary, one can elucidate the actions of some characters in *V.* by knowing at which place on history's curve they would be most at home.

Instead of a few metaphorical comments about the Jacobean age, *The Crying of Lot 49* presents an account of a pseudo-Jacobean tragedy that Pynchon has invented. *The Courier's Tragedy* does indeed have all the earmarks of that age. The narrator accurately calls it "the landscape of evil Richard

Wharfinger had fashioned for his 17th-century audiences, so preapocalyptic, death-wishful, sensually fatigued, unprepared, a little poignantly, for that abyss of civil war that had been waiting, cold and deep, only a few years ahead of them" (p. 44). The play's account of the machinations at an Italian court illustrates all these qualities. This quotation also indicates that the English Civil War will both mark the end of the cycle of which the Jacobean era is the last stage and begin a new cycle.

Because the two periods have much in common, the account of the Jacobean era in *The Crying of Lot 49* casts light on the contemporary era, during which the novel's main action occurs. Like Jacobean England, according to one character, contemporary society is at the end of a cycle. In *V.* Fausto, thinking of his development during certain periods of his life, asks, "Decadence, decadence. What is it? Only a clear movement toward death or, preferably, non-humanity" (p. 301). The war illustrates the brutality of a terminal stage, and the actions of many characters illustrate its decadence. The narrator, too, believes that the era is terminal; he calls the war a fatal disease (p. 433).

Pynchon also mentions the point of the sine curve of history that determines the curve's shape. This point and the curve's equation together indicate how the curve must be drawn. Tensor analysis, from which he also makes other metaphors, is relevant to this part of his discussion of history. The narrator of *Gravity's Rainbow* speculates that "if tensor analysis is good enough for turbulence, it ought to be good enough for history. There ought to be nodes, critical points . . . there ought to be super-derivatives of the crowded and insatiate flow that can be set equal to zero and these critical points found" (p. 451). In other words, history has crucial points that for long periods of time determine its direction.

Pynchon specifies the critical nodes that determine the era of World War II and the years immediately following it, and he explains the reasons for their great effect. Raymond Olderman lists the nine years before World War II during which the action of *V.* takes place and correctly mentions that most of those years prefigure the war (pp. 125–26). In *Gravity's Rainbow* it becomes clear which years Pynchon considers most important. Immediately after the disquisition on applying tensor analysis to history comes the announcement that 1904 was one determining year (pp. 451–52). It is important because "1904 was when Admiral Rozhdestvenski sailed his fleet halfway around the world to relieve Port Arthur, which put . . . Enzian on the planet, it was the year the Germans all but wiped out the Hereros, which gave Enzian some peculiar ideas about survival, it was the year the American Food and Drug people took the cocaine out of Coca-Cola, which gave us an alcoholic and death-oriented generation of Yanks ideally equipped to fight WW II, and it was the year Ludwig Prandtl proposed the boundary layer, which really got aerodynamics into business" (p. 452). The movement of the Russian fleet involved two of the major participants of the war to come; von Trotha's extermination of the Hereros looked forward to German murderousness and racial policy, and Prandtl's discovery contributed to two of the war's major weapons: the airplane and the rocket. Anyone who recognized the significance of these events and had traced the flow of history could have predicted the war. This theory of history goes a long way toward explaining Pynchon's novels, for he describes these events of 1904 in order to make sense of later events.

By drawing a circle, one can graph the cyclical theory of history, which some of Pynchon's characters accept. Signor Mantissa in *V.*, an Italian, thinks that he repeats Machiavelli's exile in the midst of a decaying society. He conceives this theory simply: "History would continue to recapitulate the same patterns" (p. 145). Some of the Maltese who understand their own history, that endless repetition of conquests, believe this theory, and the horror of Malta's history vivifies their conception of the theory. Even the Maltese children imagine a visual model of history: "A wheel, this diagram: Fortune's wheel. Spin as it might the basic arrangement was constant. . . . The old cyclic idea of history had taught only the rim, to which princes and serfs alike were lashed; that wheel was oriented vertical; one rose and fell. But the children's wheel was dead-level, its own rim only that of the sea's horizon—so sensuous, so 'visual' a race are we Maltese" (p. 317). Mantissa's speculations are self-serving. Little better than a common criminal, he does not even approach the stature of

Machiavelli, so his theorizing serves merely as evidence of his arrogance. The Maltese children's theory also helps delineate them by dramatizing their intellectual originality and imagination despite adversity. In addition, their theory explains Maltese history and places in a context the events on Malta in *V.*

In *Gravity's Rainbow* repetitions occur but no one explicitly develops a cyclical theory of history, partly because the characters do not notice the repetitions. For example, Osbie Feel in one scene carries a peculiar heavy gun. Answering questions about it, he says, " 'Am I going to let the extra weight make a difference? It's my *crotchet*' " (p. 107). Four pages later Pynchon describes events that happen during the seventeenth century on Mauritius. Frans Van der Groov hunts dodoes there with a huge gun but " 'he didn't mind the extra weight, it was *his* crotchet' " (p. 111). Frans also tried earlier to convert the dodoes to Christianity, which virtually repeats the attempts in *V.* of Father Fairing to convert the rats in the New York sewers. Slothrop's escapades as Plechazunga, the pig-hero, recapitulate his Puritan ancestor's swineherding and suggest that history repeats itself, the second occurrence being comic. Joseph W. Slade thinks that Pynchon may have borrowed from Carl Jung, Wolfgang Pauli and Paul Kammerer the notion of synchronicity: two causally unrelated events can have the same meaning (*Thomas Pynchon*, pp. 236–37).

A historiographer must deal with a third fundamental issue, the identity of the forces that cause historical change. Pynchon presents several different possibilities. One, the technocratic theory, appears in *Gravity's Rainbow*. Walter von Rathenau, the brilliant German administrator, says through a medium at a séance, " 'All talk of cause and effect is secular history, and secular history is a diversionary tactic. . . . If you want the truth . . . you must look into the technology of these matters. Even into the hearts of certain molecules—it is they after all which dictate temperatures, pressures, rates of flow, costs, profits, the shapes of towers' " (p. 167). The rocket's importance in this novel lends credence to Rathenau's argument. The blurring of distinctions between the warring powers also makes it appear that the technocrats on both sides use the war to advance technology, creating apparent political causes as a smoke screen.

Marxist theories of historical causation also have their defenders in Pynchon's novels. A minor character in *V.*, Kholsky, conceives of history as the product only of material objects that cause economic changes, which in turn increase "Socialist Awareness" (pp. 380–81). Since Socialist Awareness has little prominence in this novel, one suspects that Pynchon does not accept Kholsky's theory. In *Gravity's Rainbow* a looser Marxist interpretation is more convincing. Not bothering with orthodox Marxism's rigorous materialism, Katje believes that "the real business of the War is buying and selling" (p. 105). She further claims that the presence of death causes people to hunger for material goods and to reduce everything, including other humans, to market terms. As Slothrop begins to understand the commercial web woven around the rocket, he begins to see justification for this vaguely Marxist conception of the war. He learns, for example, that the Germans are using a Dutch Shell transmitter to help them aim rockets and that these rockets have propulsion systems like the ones that British Shell built. Furthermore, Duncan Sandys, Churchill's son-in-law and the man who receives all the rocket intelligence, works at Shell Mex House (p. 251). In other words, Shell operates on both the German and the British sides. Other corporations may be doing the same.

Although Pynchon devotes little space to it, the Puritan theory of causation also makes sense of some events in his novels. He does not clearly state whether or not this theory is valid, whereas he does supply corroborating evidence for the technocratic and Marxist views. No Puritans even appear until his most recent novel. One Puritan character in *Gravity's Rainbow*, Slothrop's ancestor, "felt that what Jesus was for the elect, Judas Iscariot was for the Preterite. Everything in the Creation has its equal and opposite counterpart" (p. 555). This seems to be a long-forgotten idea, but in his review Richard Poirier shows that it relates to two of Pynchon's most important themes: "Puritanism is evoked [in *Gravity's Rainbow*] as an early version of the paranoia conditioning us to look for signs of Election and rendering the rest of mankind and its evidences invisible, merely so much waste" ("Rocket Power", p. 64).

A theory that an impending apocalypse causes historical change makes good sense of the events in *Gravity's Rainbow*. Both Katje and Slothrop think that the rocket's flight symbolizes history's parabolic descent toward its conclusion. Specifically, Katje thinks that the parabola symbolizes the planet's movement toward a "terminal orgasm" (p. 223). Just as the rocket's landing marks the end of its flight, so, too, does the rocket itself indicate that mankind may finally have fashioned the instrument of its own destruction. On the novel's last page Pynchon describes the rocket approaching the end of its flight, and he comments on it in apocalyptic terms in a poem. The action earlier resembles a prelude to an apocalypse. *V.*, however, ends with the destruction of Sidney Stencil, and *The Crying of Lot 49* ends with an enigma. Bleak as these two earlier novels are, they do not present much evidence that an apocalypse is imminent.

Pynchon treats comically another view of history's cause. In *V.* as Benny Profane broods on a park bench, the narrator speculates, "If he'd been the type who evolves theories of history for his own amusement, he might have said all political events . . . have the desire to get laid as their roots; because history unfolds according to economic forces and the only reason anybody wants to get rich is so he can get laid steadily, with whomever he chooses" (p. 198). Profane, out of work and sexually frustrated, may indeed arrive at such a conclusion, and the narrator had just reported that Profane equates wealth and sex. This theory, however, reveals more about Profane than about history. Although Profane's theory comically integrates Marxism and Freudianism, Pynchon's work offers some evidence to support Profane's theory that the armature of history is sex. In other words, this brief reference designed to be taken less than seriously does explain much of the action of these novels. Its comic qualities make it unusual among Pynchon's statements on historiography. Usually such passages have an earnest tone, for his characters try desperately to find ways to understand events they cannot control.

All these theories of history fail to explain fully the historical events in Pynchon's novels. As Richard Wasson claims, "The point of [*V.*] is to reveal the inadequacy of all metaphors of history, whether they be cycles, waves, spirals or still points."[6] Like James Dean Young, he claims that the metaphors fail because they try to force data into patterns too restrictive to contain them. In addition, Pynchon presents several theories, all of which have some explanatory value, thereby implying that none by itself adequately explains the data. One must look at other fields of knowledge as well.

5.

Religion

Like the intellectual domains analyzed so far, religion plays two roles in Pynchon's work. It is the source of details used to develop characters, to advance the plot, and in general to tell the stories. Religion's importance in this regard has been overemphasized, mainly because of overzealous myth criticism. However, religion is vital to his work because two religious world views—those of the Puritans and the Hereros, or more generally an occult view— form one of the most important contrasts he has presented. This contrast is made vividly in the song at the end of *Gravity's Rainbow*, which, with the succeeding brief invitation for everyone to sing, is the last word that we presently have from Pynchon.

Some of the religious details in Pynchon's novels appear in conjunction with the theme of revelation, of characters searching for hidden meanings. James Nohrnberg, for example, finds some allusions to the Holy Ghost and annunciation, such as references to "Paracletian politics" in *V*. and to a "zany Paraclete" in *The Crying of Lot 49*.[1] Unfortunately, these seem to be random details and do not lead to a religious interpretation that significantly illuminates the novels. In the same volume of essays on Pynchon, Edward Mendelson comments, more helpfully, on religion in relation to this theme. He finds in *The Crying of Lot 49* a comment by the narrator about a "religious instant" that Oedipa has when she sees a hieroglyph inside a transistor radio (p. 118). Mendelson points out that in the next paragraph, as she reacts to the hieroglyph of her hometown stretched out beneath her, she is described as feeling "some promise of hierophany." In other words, according to Mendelson, she feels that something latent and meaningful, which later she believes to be the Tristero, may exist. He continues that "hierophany" appears to have been invented by Mircea Eliade, who expands most fully on the word in his *Patterns in Comparative Religion* but gives a more straightforward definition in his introduction to *The Sacred and the Profane*: " 'to designate the *act of manifestation* of the sacred, we have proposed the term *Hierophany*' " (p. 122). Tracing this term to Eliade is useful, since he is also a source of other important concepts that Pynchon adopts.

Critics have argued that mythic themes appear in Pynchon's work; one can find in it a few specific allusions to myths. Pynchon mentions, for example, Slothrop's "Eurydice-obsession, this *bringing back out of*" (p. 472). This obsession suits the Zone, the infernal area left after the war ended, a burnt-out region full of burnt-out people. Other evidences of mythic themes are the comparison of a harmonica player to Orpheus, and the end of the novel, in the Orpheus Movie Theater in Los Angeles. Pynchon also makes several allusions to Rilke's *Sonnets to Orpheus*. Pointsman has a mystic yearning, too: "Here's the door, one he's imagined so often in lonely Thesean brushings down his polished corridors of years: an exit out of the orthodox-Pavlovian, showing him vistas of Norrmalm, Södermalm, Deer Park and Old City" (p. 141). These localities are in Stockholm, to which Pointsman dreams of fleeing. Pynchon's metaphor depicts a man who wants to leave a labyrinth that Pavlovian psychology has built. Passing references to myth such as these, however, are not especially significant when compared to other aspects of his work.

Raymond Olderman convincingly elucidates the role of myth in the novels: "Pynchon, like other novelists of the sixties, mocks the whole tired idea of an identity search by putting the jargon we have evolved to describe that search into the mouths of the *Time-Magazine*-reading, fashionable decadents called the Whole Sick

Crew" (p. 127). This statement recognizes the context, particularly the tone, of supposedly mythic elements in Pynchon's novels.
Olderman, however, thinks that Pynchon, like the other novelists
he discusses, retells the myths that T.S. Eliot brought together in
The Waste Land. But one needs to remember that Eliot's work has
something for nearly everyone; it bristles with pegs on which to
hang analyses of other works. Olderman's reading of Pynchon
nearly always convinces when he does not let the central thesis of
his own book intrude, but that central thesis lacks the specificity
that is needed for an explanation of Pynchon's books.

Two other critics find another mythic strain in Pynchon's
work: allusions to goddesses that seem to have been influenced by
Robert Graves's *The White Goddess* and James Frazer's *The
Golden Bough.* Joseph Slade notes the familiarity of Mehmet, a
character in *V.*, with such goddesses as Astarte and Venus (p. 76).
Slade connects Graves to two important details in *V.*: "Robert
Graves has identified a comb as an essential accessory of the White
Goddess, and asserts that 'Botticelli's *Birth of Venus* is an exact
icon of her cult' " (p. 62). Building on Slade's contention, Joseph
Fahy mentions several details that Pynchon's novel has in
common with these two compendia of myth.[2] Indeed, the figure of
V. resembles a goddess. The problem, however, is that all three
books have so many details that similarities between the
compilations of myth and the novel are nearly inevitable and such
comparisons do not add much to one's understanding of
Pynchon. Moreover, as George Levine points out in *Mindful
Pleasures*, "Pynchon denies resolution into myth by wandering
among all the available myths" (p. 114). Although Levine uses
"myth" in a broader sense than do the critics who make mythic
analyses of Pynchon, he is correct that merely trying to
demonstrate mythic correlations greatly oversimplifies Pynchon.

The details about the Puritans in *Gravity's Rainbow* are much
more revealing because they point toward the Puritans' world
view, which is one of the most important concepts in the book.
Pynchon makes much of Slothrop's Puritan ancestry and
discusses the influence of that religion on the modern world. One
example is a reference to "a Puritan reflex of seeking other orders
behind the visible, also known as paranoia" (p. 188). In his article

on Puritanism and *Gravity's Rainbow* Joseph Krafft comments on this reflex: "The Puritans—the given exemplars of interpretation in the past—believed that what was 'here'—the material order, nature—was metaphoric for what was 'out there'—the spiritual order, supernature."[3] Both obsession with looking beyond the visible and paranoia are rampant among Pynchon's characters, including even some of the positive ones such as Oedipa Maas and the Hereros. These psychological problems perhaps can be traced to the Puritans' dualism (nature and supernature). They believed that supernature was reserved for them, the Elect, and that others, even such renegade Puritans as Slothrop's ancestor William, were Preterites who were unworthy of good treatment. The results of this view can be disturbing social doctrines and predatory capitalism, as Max Weber, Norman O. Brown, and others contend. Another result is the belief that nature has no intrinsic value, which allows its exploitation by scientists and others. Thus, many of the problems described in *Gravity's Rainbow* can be traced to Puritanism.

The Hereros and some believers in occult phenomena in *Gravity's Rainbow* hold a world view that may be called pantheism. They believe, like the Puritans, that there is latent meaning in visible objects but, unlike the Puritans, they believe that this fact makes the objects more valuable, not less valuable. The Hereros are most determined to find hidden meanings in the rocket:

> Say we *are* supposed to be the Kabbalists out here, say that's our real Destiny, to be the scholar-magicians of the Zone, with somewhere in it a Text, to be picked to pieces, annotated, explicated, and masturbated till it's *all* squeezed limp of its last drop . . . well we assumed—natürlich—that this holy Text had to be the Rocket, orururumo orunene the high, rising, dead, the blazing, the great one. . . . Its symmetries, its latencies, the *cuteness* of it enchanted and seduced us while the real Text persisted. (p. 520)

The rocket resembles a primitive sun god, a suitable deity for an agricultural, tropical people, but their consideration of it also as a text denotes a more sophisticated kind of religion.

Pynchon discovered the Hereros while doing research on Malta for *V.*, and he later wrote to Thomas F. Hirsch about this experience. Joseph W. Slade discusses his letter to Hirsch, thereby explaining a good deal about the anti-Puritan world view in *Gravity's Rainbow*:

> One cannot think of the Hereros without reference to their religion, Pynchon told his correspondent, for thanks to that religion, which stresses an unified and integrated tribal life and a pantheistic approach to the universe, the pre-literate, pre-colonialized, pre-rationalized Hereros view the world as a metaphysical whole. Within that world paradox is the law of experience: opposites can be individual selves yet parts of the larger self, members of a human and a cosmic community. Natural energies may be subject to entropy in such a world, but randomness is merely one aspect of the changing, cyclical order of things, as divine as the rest.[4]

Thus, the Hereros give impressive answers to many of the questions that vex Pynchon's other characters not only in *Gravity's Rainbow* but also in his other fictional works.

Pynchon usually develops a close analogue of the Hereros' religion, belief in the occult, by contrasting it to scientific world views. For example, in *Gravity's Rainbow* the White Visitation group is composed of zany occultists as well as materialistic, behavioristic scientists. This contrast may seem strange, but in the light of certain developments in the history of science it is appropriate: for centuries an occult tradition played a prominent role in German science.[5] As the sciences developed and became more rigorous, this strain diminished, replaced by mechanistic, empiricist science. In *Gravity's Rainbow* the occult tradition reappears not among the Germans but, ironically, in response to the rocket, the most destructive product of their technology, and among the Hereros, some members of the White Visitation, and others.

Paracelsus, the sixteenth-century alchemist—or, as he called himself, iatrochemist—is the most important early figure in the occult tradition. He believed that scientists could create imitations of naturally occurring substances; in this he resembles the scientists in Pynchon's novel who attempt synthesis. He believed, too, that all substances are alive, which is the most important part of this tradition that Pynchon uses. The dominant scientific position among Pynchon's characters is that substances are dead, a view that has prevailed in British science, partly because it accords with the empirical bent of British philosophy and Newtonian mechanism. In *Gravity's Rainbow* Pynchon thus turns the history of science on its head. The Germans, lacking reverence for nature, in spite of the iatrochemical tradition, threaten the British with the rocket. The minority position holds that substances are alive, and in the context of a war this distinction becomes crucial because it raises moral issues about the military uses of technology.

The life of a substance, according to Paracelsus, derived from the Archeus, the vital force, within it. This, like the basis of the Hereros' religion, is a pantheistic idea and has moral and political implications. If all things have this vital spirit, they are therefore autonomous and hierarchies are illegitimate. The characters in the lower end of the hierarchies in this novel, those who seek freedom, naturally prefer a theory of nature and a type of science that suits their political aspirations. Knowledge is attained, Paracelsus concluded, by participating in the free spiritual realm and by thus getting in touch with the Archeus in things. In other words, he advocated a mystical epistemology like that of some of Pynchon's characters. Because the Archeus survives death, rebirth is possible. The rebirth-through-death theme appears often and importantly in the works of Paracelsus, as it does in *Gravity's Rainbow*. Friedman and Puetz, for example, have found seventeen instances in that novel of what they call "the compost-garden image" (p. 348). Unfortunately, this conception can be used to excuse murder and destruction.

The opposite theory, that nature is a machine rather than a spiritual entity, dominated science for centuries. The vitalistic German tradition, however, recurred in the works of Boehme and Leibnitz. Pynchon refers occasionally to the latter. Like Paracelsus, Boehme believed in the spiritual nature of reality. He held, as did Swedenborg and many later Romantics, that nature was spirit externalized and he also agreed with Paracelsus that strife and eventual death led to rebirth in a higher form. Similarly,

Leibnitz's monads, which he considered to be the building blocks of the world, were centers of vital, spiritual force.

These ideas flowered later in nineteenth-century German Nature Philosophy.[5] Herder, for example, believed in evolutionary progress through death and rebirth. Schelling and Oken, who systematized these ideas, also conceived of a World Spirit. Oken was a dualist in the sense that he viewed polarity as the fundamental creative condition. The main conflict, he thought, is between an individualizing, vital process and a universalizing, destructive one. Many of the characters in *Gravity's Rainbow* perceive the world in this way. Oken thought that all living things had in common not only the World Spirit but also "infusorial mucus-vesicles," which were material entities, an idea that is a precursor of cell theory.

The Nature Philosophers had their greatest impact on the biological sciences, particularly embryology and morphology, and on evolutionary thought and cell theory. They had less influence on the physical sciences, but occasionally their anti-mechanism challenged the dominant physical theories. Goethe, for example, disagreeing with Newton, thought that colors were not contained in white light but were produced by the interaction of light and darkness. As evidence he cited the afterimages of the sun that one sees after moving quickly from sunlight into a dark room. Goethe's premise is that the images produced by the living eye are just as valid as objective images produced outside the eye. As he put it, "optical illusion is optical truth." His theory thus supplies still another meaning for the scene in *Gravity's Rainbow* that describes the barbed wire on the beach. The Nature Philosophers, because of their belief in the importance of polarities, were also interested in electricity and magnetism, two topics that are important in Pynchon's work.

Schleiden and Schwann built cell theory on the foundation of Nature Philosophy. Schwann thought that growth resulted from a vital force inside cells attracting new molecules. Virchow applied cell theory to pathology, holding that individual cells were the locus of disease. He characteristically expressed his views in social analogies, for example likening the cell to an individual who retains his identity and much of his freedom and likening the body to a society. Virchow's theories are thus relevant to the struggle of individuals in *Gravity's Rainbow*. Against this notion of the autonomy of individual parts stands Pavlov, a major figure in *Gravity's Rainbow*, who argues that the integrating function of the nervous system decreased the importance and autonomy of individual cells. The political analogue of this kind of human system is totalitarianism.

Another German scientist, Weismann, is related tangentially to the Nature Philosophers through his emphasis on the effect of individual parts. He should be mentioned here, because he has almost the same last name as Captain Blicero (Weissmann) and because later thinkers twisted his genetic theories into the racial doctrines that led to some of the sufferings described in *V.* and *Gravity's Rainbow*. The slight change in names is significant because Weismann means "wise man" and Weissmann means "white man." He distinguished between germ plasm, which transmitted hereditary characteristics, and body plasm; he even established that the germ plasm lay on the chromosomes. He gave inheritance much more importance than environment and viewed humans as less subject to variation. Gobineau, a Frenchman, and Chamberlain, an Englishman, derived racist theories from Weismann's work. Pynchon probably was alluding to this line of thought when he named a German in *V.* Weissmann, but the relation of it to Captain Blicero (Weissmann's name in *Gravity's Rainbow*) is less clear, since Blicero's attachment to Enzian, a Black, seems to dilute the racist theory.

Since the time of Paracelsus this tradition in German science has gradually become more differentiated from the occult, although the two schools of thought have several of the same premises. Pynchon refers more often specifically to the latter school than to the former, which is often implicitly relevant. An understanding of this aspect of German science will, however, clarify some of the incidental details in Pynchon's novels and also, by revealing the intellectual antecedents, his references to the occult.

Some characters in Pynchon's work who believe in the occult regard almost everything as a symbol. For example, "Eddie is a connoisseur of shivers. He is even able, in some strange way, to *read* them, like Säure Bummer reads reefers, like Miklos Thanatz reads whip-scars" (p. 641). The narrator even proposes an elaborate occult explanation of gravity:

> Gravity, taken so for granted, is really something eerie, Messianic, extrasensory in Earth's mindbody . . . having hugged to its holy center the wastes of dead species, gathered, packed, transmuted, realigned, and rewoven molecules to be taken up again by the coal-tar Kabbalists of the other side, the ones Bland on his voyages has noted, taken boiled off, teased apart, explicated to every last permutation of useful magic, centuries past exhaustion still finding new molecular pieces, combining and recombining them into new synthetics. (p. 590)

Here he demonstrates a new way of understanding the recurrent waste and death in this novel. His nonscientific theory offers a vitalistic explanation of molecular combinations and opposes the syntheses of the organic chemists, whose dyes and plastics worry proponents of the occult. In general, occultism supports old notions against modern science's onslaught; it advocates learning from nature, for example, not manipulating and modifying it. The occult thus is a rallying point for those who oppose modern society and its scientific orientation. In this context, the rocket represents the thrust of science up and out of a magical world view, taking with it modern culture. The occult view of gravity is original and explicates a force few would think amenable to any explanation but a scientific one.

In *Gravity's Rainbow* Pynchon alludes more often to the Tarot than to any other occult system. Arthur Edward Waite serves as an appropriate explicator of this system.[6] A Tarot pack contains four suits: Wands, Cups, Swords, and Pentacles. Each suit has cards numbered from one to ten and a King, Queen, Knave (sometimes called a Page), and Knight. In addition there are Trumps Major: Magician, High Priestess, Empress, Emperor, High Priest, Lovers, Chariot, Fortitude, Hermit, Wheel of Fortune, Justice, Hanged Man, Death, Temperance, Devil, Tower Struck by Lightning, Star, Moon, Sun, Last Judgment, World, and Fool. Of the last of those cards Edward Mendelson makes an interesting point: "Slothrop is gradually reduced to his final emblem: the Fool in the Tarot deck, the only card without a number, lacking a place in the systems of the world."[7] The existence of various systems of interpretation, some of them linked with other arcana such as the Kabbala, the richness and ambiguity of the symbolism, and the reticence of Tarot practitioners have combined to shroud this pack of cards in mystery. The symbolism's richness, most relevant here, attracted T.S. Eliot of course, *The Waste Land* being the most famous literary work that alludes to the Tarot. That poem also demonstrates the pack's ambiguity. The Hanged Man appears threatening in *The Waste Land*, but Waite calls it a positive card. The intricate pictures on the cards also create ambiguity. One could, for example, draw an analogy between the serpent that devours its tail and circles the waist of the Magician and the infinite serpent in Kekulé's dream that showed him the structure of the benzene ring.

Although Waite opposes using the cards for fortune-telling, he explains a Celtic method of divination based on them, which Pynchon incorporates into *Gravity's Rainbow*. After a brief, cryptic explanation of Slothrop's fortune as revealed by the cards, Pynchon uses the pack to tell Weissmann's fortune (p. 746 ff.). He gives a full and satisfactory explanation of the Crowning, Beneath, Behind, Self, and House cards but not of the others. The Significator, the only card in fortune-telling not selected at random, represents a man over forty with dark hair and hazel or gray eyes. Although Pynchon does not mention this meaning, this card gives the first indication of Weissmann's appearance. Pynchon, however, does discuss the martial symbolism of the Knight, which suits Weissmann. The Covering card, as he mentions, represents the subject's present condition. The Rocket is a good interpretation of the Tower, because it means, according to Waite, ruin, the materialization of the spiritual, and the fall of false doctrine. The second of these qualities becomes particularly significant in light of the passage about the occult interpretation of gravity, which fits it perfectly. The Crossing card, the main obstacle, turns out to be the Queen of Swords. This usually means female sadness, separation, or mourning, but Pynchon writes that here it may represent Weissmann dressed in drag, as he is during part of *V*. Waite, but not Pynchon, writes that the Four of Cups, the Before (immediate future) card, connotes aversion and disgust. The card showing What Will Come, the World, has more complexities than Pynchon cites. It signifies a perfect world and thus, although obscure, provides this novel's most optimistic statement.

The notion that time is cyclical appeals to the Hereros, to some of the occultists, and to other characters, as belief in linear time appeals to the scientists. A quotation from Rilke, "once, only once," sums up the linear conception of time. Believers of that conception can deduce that " 'if we are here once, only once, then clearly we are here to take what we can while we may' " (p. 539). However, a crucial event in the history of science, Kekulé's visualization of the shape of the benzene molecule, which he achieved during a dream about a serpent swallowing its tail, suggests the alternative view of time. In one of the most important passages in *Gravity's Rainbow* Pynchon alludes to that dream and mentions some of the implications of both conceptions of time:

> The Serpent that announces, "The World is a closed thing, cyclical, resonant, eternally-returning," is to be delivered into a system whose only aim is to *violate* the Cycle. Taking and not giving back, demanding that "productivity" and "earnings" keep on increasing with time, the System removing from the rest of the World these vast quantities of energy to keep its own tiny desperate fraction showing a profit: and not only most of humanity—most of the world, animal, vegetable and mineral, is laid waste in the process. (p. 412)

Pynchon makes two other important points about these theories of time and their implications. First, " 'to believe that each of Them *will* personally die is also to believe that Their system will die—that some chance of renewal, some dialectic, is still operating in History. To affirm Their mortality is to affirm Return' " (p. 540). For a while there was reason to hope that America was the instrument of Return that would defeat Them: "America was a gift from the invisible powers, a way of returning. But Europe refused it" (p. 722). In fact, "American Death has come to occupy Europe." Mircea Eliade, one of the major sources of *Gravity's Rainbow*, explains some of the other implications of these two theories of time.

Many of these religious themes are recapitulated in the cryptic poem that concludes *Gravity's Rainbow*, describing an apocalypse during which the proponents of linear time are replaced by the proponents of cyclical time. The first line of the poem refers to a Hand, a type of deity, turning the time: converting it from linear time to cyclical time. Meanwhile the Towers, which, as the Tarot fortune-telling passage indicates, represent the rocket, are brought low. The same force that accomplishes this, a Light, will "find the last poor Pret'rite one," probably to preserve him or her, for the Preterites will inherit the earth after the Elect and Their rocket are destroyed. The Riders, probably the four horsemen of the apocalypse, will sleep, their work being finished. The poem ends by describing the pantheistic world that will remain:

With a face on ev'ry mountainside,
And a Soul in ev'ry stone. . . .(p.760)

6.

The Film

The film is the only artistic medium except literature that plays an important role in Pynchon's short stories and novels. As with the other disciplines, he presents information about the film and examines its methods of organizing information. As to the information, he occasionally mentions popular films, but his references to them are usually obvious and of little importance. Much more important are the references in *Gravity's Rainbow* to classic German films. As to film's methods of organizing information, as he does with history, Pynchon analyzes the nature of film. Virtually all of the important examples appear in *Gravity's Rainbow*, subtly worked into the narrative.

Siegfried Kracauer's *From Caligari to Hitler* provides the best account of the early German film industry.[1] In fact, his contention that these films most clearly reveal German mass ideology and thus explain the susceptibility of many Germans to Nazism fits perfectly with Pynchon's attempt to explain Nazism's etiology. So many echoes of Kracauer's book appear in *Gravity's Rainbow* that the reader is led to believe that Pynchon almost certainly has read it; the only other possibility is that he has independently learned about these films. In either case, Kracauer's book illuminates many important parts of this novel.

132

Kracauer notes the motif of the double in an important film made by Hanns Ewers before World War I. In *The Student of Prague* (1913), "borrowing from E. T. A. Hoffmann, the Faust legend and Poe's story 'William Wilson,' Ewers presents us with the poor student Baldwin signing a compact with the queer sorcerer Scapinelli" (p. 29). As his part of the bargain Scapinelli becomes the student's mirror reflection. The little-known Ewers is significant mainly for popularizing this motif. After World War I, doubles proliferated, and the changing use of the motif symbolizes for Kracauer a dangerous drift toward totalitarianism: "Just before the war, *The Student of Prague* had mirrored the duality of any liberal under the Kaiser; now [1923] *The Street* foreshadowed a duality provoked by the retrogressive move from rebellion to submission" (p. 123). Kracauer then cites four other significant films produced between 1920 and 1931 that use doubles. This tracing of motifs and psychological analysis typifies Kracauer's method. As has been discussed, Pynchon also uses doubles.

The Cabinet of Dr. Caligari (1920), Kracauer contends, more than any other film reveals the dangerous forces in the German sensibility. He attributes special significance to a change made by Weine after Janowitz and Mayer turned over to him control of this remarkable film. The original directors cast Caligari as a symbol of lust after power and unlimited authority, and Cesare, the instrument of Caligari, as "the common man who, under pressure of compulsory military service, is drilled to kill and to be killed" (p. 65). The hero, Francis, finally discovers that the director of the insane asylum to which Caligari was sent had assumed Caligari's identity. This unmasking, Kracauer argues, represents the beneficial triumph of reason over irrational authority. This triumph, however, ran counter to the anti-rational tendencies that, as Mosse shows in his analysis of German ideology, were dominant at that time. In Weine's version of the film, however, Francis is the madman, and he mistakes the asylum's director for Caligari. In fact, a frame story reveals that Francis has imagined Caligari. This change reverses the film's meaning: "The original story exposed the madness inherent in authority, Weine's *Caligari* glorified authority and convicted its antagonist of madness" (p. 67). Kracauer inadvertently states here what turns out to be the most important moral and psychological question in Pynchon's work: is authority dangerous and resistance therefore not only justified but also obligatory, or is authority benign and resistance therefore a symptom of paranoia? Stencil, Oedipa, Slothrop, and a host of minor characters struggle with this conundrum.

A little later, in the early 1920s, Ernst Lubitsch became an important filmmaker. Most of his early films describe the individual's struggle against the masses, thereby revealing, according to Kracauer, the strong anti-democratic sentiment rampant in Germany (p. 55 ff.). In *Gravity's Rainbow* many individuals—Slothrop, Mexico, Enzian, and others—stand alone, but not against the masses, which also are victimized, but against an enigmatic enemy. After these early films, Lubitsch turned to gigantic historical films designed to prove that great people, rather than other causes, make history. For instance, his film about Madame du Barry totally ignores the social and economic causes of the French Revolution and attributes it to the psychological traits of the powerful. These films belong to the authoritarian tradition in the German cinema and, since they were ahistorical, also helped the Germans forget World War I. Kracauer explains Lubitsch's success by remarking that "the majority of people lived in fear of social changes and therefore welcomed films which defamed not only bad rulers but also good revolutionary causes" (p. 53). Hitler also learned to take advantage of this fear of change. The few Nazis described by Pynchon are authoritarian, and one (Weissmann) thinks that another (Katje) "secretly . . . fears the Change" (p. 97).

The career of G. W. Pabst clarifies both the German sensibility as Pynchon depicts it and the power of a German film company, Ufa, to which Pynchon refers. First, three of Pabst's films, released in 1928 and 1929, depict the relationship between "social disintegration and sexual excesses," a familiar theme in all three of Pynchon's novels (p. 178). Second, Ufa distorted some of Pabst's films, changing one perhaps in order to take "pleasure in elaborating upon the embarrassments of a democracy" (p. 174). Ufa dominated German filmmaking, partly by catering in this way to political sentiments. Kracauer considers its influence evil, both artistically and politically, and Pynchon echoes the political part of this charge, depicting Ufa as another too-powerful corporation like IG Farben, not as a benevolent distributor of art.

The films of Fritz Lang provide further clues to Pynchon's books. His first important film, *Destiny*, was released in 1921. Pynchon refers to its German title, *Der Müde Tod*. The Angel of Death, Fate's agent, appears in it, and three episodes set in widely different times and places form intercalated dream sequences. This film ends with a young woman following her lover to death, but its real significance lies in the actions of Death, which triumphs in both the frame story and all three intercalated episodes. "This plot forces one point strongly on the audience," writes Kracauer, "that, however arbitrary they seem, the actions of tyrants are realizations of Fate" (p. 90). By having Fate perform homely actions Lang humanizes it and thus makes its control seem benevolent. He also carefully demonstrates that Fate will always have its way; for example, in one of the dream episodes a couple flees ponderously, but Fate causes their pursuers to move even more ponderously. This film encouraged some Germans to accept a ruler whom they could identify with fate. Total control of the sort that such a ruler would have is of course a central theme in Pynchon's work. Although none of his characters believes in a benevolent fate, many of them believe that something controls them. His frequent references to this attitude, especially in *Gravity's Rainbow*, and his allusions to Lang make a strong case for his borrowing from that film director.

The next important Lang film, *Dr. Mabuse, the Gambler* (1922), features a main character who is rather Pynchonesque, in that his lust for power leads him from depravity to madness (p. 81 ff.). Lang released it two years after *The Cabinet of Dr. Caligari*, which it resembles. Both films document the relationship of power to madness and use circle imagery to express chaos. Some of Pynchon's characters resemble Dr. Mabuse, whose power, although omnipresent, is unknown to most people. Of the actor who played Mabuse, Pynchon writes in *Gravity's Rainbow*, "You were meant to think of Hugo Stinnes, the tireless operator behind the scenes of apparent Inflation, apparent history" (p. 579).

Kracauer sees political implications in Lang's film, because in it, as in *The Cabinet of Dr. Caligari*, chaos and tyranny form an inescapable dichotomy like those that vex Pynchon's characters.

Ironically, *The Nibelungen* (1924), Lang's next important film, played into Hitler's hands (p. 91 ff.). Lang made this film to publicize German culture, which later was also a purpose of the propaganda of Goebbels. The Nazis, in fact, adopted some of *The Nibelungen*'s images. It is possible that Pynchon used as a source this version of Teutonic myth rather than medieval legends or Wagner's operas. Whatever his source, he refers occasionally to characters in heroic medieval costume, the Plechazunga episode parodies Germanic myth, and the Liebestod motif comes from one of these sources. Pynchon refers to this film in *Gravity's Rainbow*, but despite these possible borrowings, *The Nibelungen* has less relevance to Pynchon than do Lang's other major films (p. 159).

Pynchon's books show important similarities with one of Lang's most famous films, *Metropolis* (1927). At the center of the film, too, stands a powerful character who controls nearly everyone else. This man, an industrialist, dominates his workers and the rest of the metropolis. When threatened by an uprising, he becomes manipulative in order to triumph. For instance, he craftily builds a robot in the form of a woman who has been trying to organize the workers. The inanimate but semihuman objects in Pynchon's books, such as SHROUD, resemble this robot. Something in this film, probably the triumph of authority, impressed the Nazis. Goebbels told Lang that "many years before [Hitler's rise], he and the Führer had seen . . . *Metropolis* in a small town, and Hitler had said at that time that he wanted [Lang] to make the Nazi pictures" (p. 164). In *Gravity's Rainbow* Pynchon mentions an actor, an actress, and a scene from this film (p. 578).

The other film of Lang's that is most famous, *M* (1931), also interested the Nazis, but for very different reasons. Some party officials thought that its original title, *Murderer among Us*, referred to Hitler. Its central character succumbs to the violent, anarchic forces within himself and murders a child. Lang thus modifies the tradition of the double. The murder's immaturity, evident in the facial features of the young Peter Lorre, who played the part, makes him unable to resist these impulses. He belongs at the anarchy pole of the dichotomy that recurs in German films of this era, and his resulting brutality implies that he should have accepted authority, the other pole. Like *M*, Pynchon's novels describe this dichotomy and contain characters whose latent violence perpetually threatens to become manifest.

Pynchon also develops themes found in some of Lang's other films. The plot of *Gravity's Rainbow* has some elements in common with that of *The Woman in the Moon* (1929), which describes a rocket trip. Pynchon alludes to that film a few times; once two characters see it and another time the narrator reports that for it Lang invented the countdown. Von Braun and Ordway consider Lang's film important enough to rocketry to mention it in their *History of Rocketry and Space Travel*. They write that Hermann Oberth, Germany's leading rocket expert at the time, served as technical director of the film and tried unsuccessfully to launch a rocket as a publicity stunt. Peter Bogdanovich adds that Willy Ley, another famous rocket scientist, also advised the makers of *The Woman in the Moon*.[2] Paul M. Jensen writes that two other rocket experts, Skershevsky, a Russian, and Rudolf Nebel, a German, helped with it.[3] In the film space travelers try to obtain gold for an international financial syndicate. Powerful syndicates also appear frequently in Pynchon's work. Although the plot of the film differs considerably from that of *Gravity's Rainbow*, Pynchon does find here a precedent for a work of art about a rocket.

Pynchon's narrator generalizes about a recurrent theme in Lang's films: "Metropolitan inventor Rothwang, King Attila, Mabuse der Spieler . . . all their yearnings aimed the same way, toward a form of death that could be demonstrated to hold joy and defiance" (p. 579). Rothwang appears in *Metropolis*, Attila appears in *The Nibelungen*, and *Mabuse der Spieler* is German for *Mabuse the Gambler*. In the passage quoted above, the characters may seem heroic; however, the name replaced by the ellipsis is Laszlo Jamf, one of Pynchon's most dangerous villains. Such an attitude toward death insures more human sacrifices for the Reich. Although the narrator praises these film characters, he does so in the context of a revery of Pökler's, who does not act on its basis. Rather, he cooperates with the Nazis only enough to preserve himself and to see his daughter.

In *Gravity's Rainbow* Pynchon combines qualities of these directors and of others to create Gerhardt von Göll, an archetypal German film director of the period between the wars. Pynchon suggests his purpose when he calls von Göll "once an intimate and still the equal of Lang, Pabst, Lubitsch" (p. 112). Von Göll's films show his similarities to these filmmakers. He plans to film the Argentinian epic poem *Martin Fierro* by José Hernandez, the first part of which appeared in 1872, after many years of governmental repression in Argentina. Pynchon rightly describes its main conflict as "central government vs. gaucho anarchism" (p. 386). In an introduction to one edition Carlos Alberto Astiz claims that in this poem "the government . . . acts always in favor of the selected few."[4] Fierro himself holds this view of the struggle, claiming that "a poor man runs out his life / Running from the authorities" (p. 21). Von Göll, however, certainly does not plan to produce anti-Nazi propaganda. In the first place, he has nearly decided to make a film of part two of the poem, in which Fierro becomes reconciled to the government. Second, the narrator calls Fierro's alternative anarchism instead of freedom. In other words, von Göll's film will exemplify the anarchy / authority dichotomy found in the films that did a great deal to make authority attractive to the German public shortly before Hitler came upon the scene.

In another film von Göll for once ran counter to the mainstream by producing a film biography of mad Ludwig II at a time when "the rage . . . was all for Frederick" (p. 394). His film oddly resembles the much later *Last Year at Marienbad* in "the gold, the mirrors, the miles of baroque ornament. . . . Especially those *long corridors*" (p. 394). The tradition of films about Frederick the Great to which Pynchon refers began in 1922 with a film directed by von Cserepy that defended a lost cause, the restoration of the German monarchy, and unwittingly also defended a cause that was yet to come—Hitler's. Kracauer claims that this film and the many others on the same subject advocated total surrender to authority. Von Göll varies this tradition to produce escapist films, "corridor madness," rather than rebellion. This film about Ludwig like his other films, fits his character. Von Göll's influence does not end with his films. Using the alias der Springer, he deals in drugs, literally changing the consciousness of people, as his films figuratively change it. His power also extends into international politics, for he is "meshed in with the affairs of any number of exile governments, fluctuations in currencies, the establishment and disestablishment of an astonishing network of market operations winking on, winking off across the embattled continent" (p. 112). He also has links with IG Farben, which sells him Emulsion J, Jamf's film stock, at reduced rates (p. 387). His political power and relations to large German companies allude to the power and connections of Ufa, which worried Kracauer. In contrast, von Göll also assists the British war effort by making a propaganda film purporting to record the activities of the Schwarzkommando, a Black German military unit. Ironically, Enzian and other Hereros form a unit of Black rocket troops opposed to the Germans. Von Göll insinuates himself into the life of Slothrop, who has fleeting sexual relationships with both von Göll's former mistress, Greta, and his stepdaughter, Bianca. Von Göll and Slothrop also both take part in a bizarre raid on Peenemünde. This intertwining of Slothrop's life with von Göll's is indicative of the wide influence of German filmmakers between the wars.

Pynchon's examination of the nature of film is extremely significant, given this art form's present importance and its interrelations with literature. Pynchon actually adapts some of its techniques for literary purposes. A clear example appears in *Gravity's Rainbow*: the representations of holes printed occasionally in this book, as Richard Poirier points out, probably represent sprocket holes like those in film ("Rocket Power," p. 60). This device implies that one should read this novel as one would view a film, which is good advice, even though Pynchon's publisher, not Pynchon, added this graphic detail. Another cinematic technique is Pynchon's ending the book with an invitation to his readers to join in singing, as did the audiences of old movie musical short features. In addition to deriving from Menippean satire, the interspersal of singing by characters in this novel derives from musical comedy. Pynchon also finds literary equivalents more sophisticated than these three for several technical devices available to filmmakers. Most notably, his quick dissolves and rapid shifting of scenes resemble the montages of Sergei Eisenstein and others. Oddly, Eisenstein has said that he learned these techniques from an earlier novelist, Dickens. Also, in the opening scene Pynchon pans cinematically around the setting. Of these borrowings, the montage technique works most effectively, but the major importance of cinematic techniques to this book is not their hints about how it should be read but their methods of organizing information.

Another book that does not mention Pynchon does explain some of these methods. Arnold Hauser's decision to title the last section of his *Social History of Art* "The Film Age" announces film's growing importance among modern art forms. About film's relation to reality Hauser makes two points that have particular importance in regard to Pynchon. First, he writes, "The most fundamental difference between the film and other arts is that, in its world-picture, the boundaries of space and time are fluid— space has a quasi-temporal, time to some extent, a spatial character" (pp. 239–40). That is, film is a series of images arranged in a temporal sequence. It thus disputes conventional notions about these two basic constituents of the everyday world view, as does Pynchon.

Pynchon cinematically manipulates time much more frequently than space, often in a specifically cinematic context. For example, Pökler thinks of his daughter's annual visits with him as a succession of frames. In film of course the succession of frames creates the illusion of movement and, therefore, of time passing. Pökler's seeing his daughter resembles taking a photograph; seeing her the next year resembles taking another. She seems to grow magically between visits, just as a flower photographed at long intervals appears to be growing rapidly. Similarly, change in nonhuman objects can be likened to frames exposed at very long intervals. About a rock's changes one character says, " 'We're talking frames per century' " (p. 612). Stopping time by freezing movement fascinated people long before the advent of film. Pynchon makes this point and relates it to Pökler's experience with his daughter: "There has been this strange connection between the German mind and the rapid flashing of successive stills to counterfeit movement, for at least two centuries—since Leibniz [*sic*], in the process of inventing calculus, used the same approach to break up the trajectories of cannonballs through the air. And now Pökler was about to be given proof that these techniques had been extended past images on film, to human lives" (p. 407). Leibnitz, who begins to seem like the archetypal German thinker, thus appears again. This German fascination with stopping time was partly responsible for the flowering of the German film industry after World War I. German rocket engineers also advanced their science by using calculus to fragment rocket trajectories.

The narrator of *Gravity's Rainbow* also connects time, film, and the rocket: "Imagine a missile one hears approaching only *after* it explodes. The reversal! A piece of time neatly snipped out . . . a few feet of film run backwards" (p. 48). Late in this novel he adds an even more imaginative connection between the rocket and time: "a controlled burning—breaking downward again, an uncontrolled explosion . . . this lack of symmetry leads to speculating that a presence, analogous to the Aether, flows through time, as the Aether flows through space" (p. 726). Here he again attacks a commonsense notion, now from two directions: contemporary technology and a long discredited, animistic idea, the two of which oddly support each other. James Clerk Maxwell, who is important for other reasons to Pynchon's work, was one of the last prominent advocates of that idea.

Hauser's second point that helps to clarify Pynchon's novels concerns film's relation to the machine. About film he writes that "the machine is its origin, its medium and its most suitable subject" (p. 256). The reference to the obvious but easily ignored fact that film, unlike nearly all other art forms, issues from a machine, the camera, and is processed and projected by other machines justifies Pynchon's speculation in *Gravity's Rainbow* about the technological aspects of filmmaking. The importance of these machines to the film industry and film's ability to depict movement, especially mechanical movement, more effectively than most other art forms support Hauser's contention that the machine is the most suitable subject for films. The impact of Eisenstein's shots of pistons in *Potemkin* also strengthens Hauser's argument. It is probably not by coincidence that *Gravity's Rainbow* both focuses on an intricate machine, the rocket, and depends heavily on the film for ideas and techniques.

In his analysis of cinematic methods Pynchon also considers film's relation to reality by describing the two impinging on each other. The shock of von Göll, who sometimes calls himself der Springer, when he learns about the Hereros constitutes one example: "Since discovering that Schwarzkommando are really in the Zone, leading real, paracinematic lives that have nothing to do with him or the phony Schwarzkommando footage he shot last winter in England for Operation Black Wing, Springer has been zooming around in a controlled ecstasy of megalomania. He is convinced that his film has somehow brought them into being" (p. 388). The word "paracinematic," an interesting touch, suggests that for von Göll film has more reality than does ordinary existence. Pynchon thereby hints at art's importance by imagining that it can create characters who will begin to exist also in the everyday world.

He also shows that film reproduces bits of objective reality more accurately than any other artistic medium. Pynchon speculates once on the possibility that film can come closer than it presently does to a complete rendering of physical reality. He imagines a new kind of film stock, " 'Emulsion' J, invented by Laszlo Jamf, which somehow was able, even under ordinary daylight, to render the human skin transparent to a depth of half a millimeter, revealing the face just beneath the surface" (p. 387). Jamf thus found a way to understand skin, an image that recurs in this novel, such as in descriptions of the Hereros and the character who can by changing his skin's chemical composition thereby change his pigmentation.

Pynchon creates two characters who derive from films less literally than von Göll thinks the Schwarzkommando derive from his film. Margherita Erdmann, an actress in von Göll's *Alpdrucken*, sexually arouses Pökler so much with her performance that he returns home and conceives Ilse (p. 397). Margherita herself conceives Bianca because of the same film when von Göll lets the cameras continue after he has finished a scene. At that time several actors have sex with Margherita, and one becomes Bianca's father. These two "film-children" have nearly opposite personalities. Pynchon here works with an idea more subtle than the banal idea that art can arouse sexual desire. The appearance of the two girls in this novel furnishes the key to the meaning of this subtle idea by showing the novelist competing in creativity with a filmmaker, whom he himself has invented. That is, Pynchon creates Ilse and Bianca and suggests that in a sense a movie also creates them. By including them he further confuses the status of the different kinds of reality in his novel. The film is doubly fictive, because Pynchon creates it and, according to the novel's norms, von Göll creates it. Like other incidents already mentioned, this intrusion into a realm that is real in terms of this novel implies that an artistic creation can intrude into the realm that people always assume is real.

Pynchon also makes a purely epistemological point about film's relation to everyday events by showing that the former can clarify the latter. Greta, a film actress, naturally uses her cinematic experience in this way. When she "hears shots out in the increasingly distant streets, she will think of the sound stages of her early career, and will take the explosions as cue calls for the titanic sets of her dreams to be smoothly clogged with a thousand extras" (p. 446). The mental process described here has a significant progression. At first she merely makes analogies, as indicated by "think of" and "take . . . as," but then she refers to "the titanic sets of her dreams." In other words, her conscious mind forms analogies between the real and the cinematic, but her unconscious mind in dreams conceives reality to be literally cinematic.

Von Göll hopes that everyone's conscious mind will someday have a structure like Greta's. When told that life differs from films, he answers, " 'Not yet. Maybe not quite yet. You'd better enjoy it while you can. Someday, when the film is fast enough, the equipment pocket-size and burdenless and selling at people's prices, the lights and booms no longer necessary, *then* . . . then . . .' " (p. 527). Then all the world will be a film stage, and life will literally be the sum of all the films that people make. Presumably, people will take films of each other taking films, thus creating a self-enclosed cinematic realm. The world of the film will intrude as far as possible into the everyday world by replacing it.

One point that Pynchon makes about film's relation to the novel resembles von Göll's prediction of the future. Pynchon begins one scene by announcing that a camera follows Katje (p. 92). He does not mean it literally; he uses this device partly for narrative purposes—to describe the setting and her actions—and partly to indicate the meanings that a camera can communicate. When she looks into the oven, "the camera records no change in her face" (p. 93). A precise description of more action follows, and "the cameraman is pleased at the unexpected effect of so much flowing crepe" (p. 94). The camera thus avoids something it cannot do—describing the contents of Katje's mind—and turns quickly to something it can do well—depicting physical objects. Pynchon then makes explicit the contrast between the capabilities of film and literature: "At the images she sees in the mirror Katje also feels a cameraman's pleasure, but knows what he cannot; that inside herself, enclosed in the *soignée* surface of dead fabric and dead cells, she is corruption and ashes, she belongs in a way none of them can guess cruelly to the Oven" (p. 94). Here traditional novelistic narrative takes over, as film fails again. To underscore the point, Pynchon writes that Katje is thinking about Hansel and Gretel, the oven having suggested to her this subject. That is, a folk tale, a kind of literature, explains Katje's thoughts when film cannot. Film of course does have techniques for revealing unexpressed thoughts, but only the voice of a narrator, the soliloquy, and certain kinds of dialogue can approach the effectiveness of literature's techniques; moreover, these techniques have been borrowed from literature.

To show, in contrast, that in some ways film can narrate as effectively as literature Pynchon inserts a miniature film script, complete with the names of actors who will play the parts (p. 534 ff.). After it ends, he substitutes one of his characters for each actor, thus demonstrating that he can use a film to narrate that part of the story. Similarly, placing some of this novel's action in a set that was built for von Göll's future production of *Martin*

Fierro suggests that each of these media effectively describes setting (p. 610 ff.). The buildings and everything in them are real, and after von Göll completes the film the sets will remain in place; hence they do have reality outside the film.

The most extensive conjunction of film and literature in *Gravity's Rainbow* occurs at the very end. The last episode opens by indicating its setting, a movie theater in which the film has been interrupted because one of the projector's bulbs has burned out at the point where the image of a rocket is frozen in the last instant before it strikes. The frames of film, which Pynchon occasionally relates to time's passage, have, by stopping, stopped time. The song that follows describes an apocalypse during which linear time stops. The last words, "now everybody—," invite the reader to join in, to become part of a movie audience. This novel, related in several ways to film, at its end thus gives the impression that it has actually been transformed into film. To reinforce his point that literature is a process, not a product, Pynchon suggests that he has transformed his work of literature into a film precisely when he finishes it, a transformation that in another sense prevents its completion.

7.

Literature

Pynchon refers frequently to other works of literature. With literature, as with history and film, he examines its nature rather than specific ways in which those who produce it have made patterns. He also shows how literature can borrow from other disciplines information and methods of organizing it. His books, even the very long *Gravity's Rainbow*, are literary organizations of information.

Most of the literary allusions in Pynchon's work are to German literature and appear in *Gravity's Rainbow*. German folk literature, the simplest kind of literature in that novel, forms part of the German ideology that George L. Mosse explains in *The Crisis of German Ideology*. Besides the *Volkish* irrationality of the German ideology, its mystical conception of physical setting, its interest in the occult, and Hans Blüher's theory of the usefulness of homosexuality to the Bund, Pynchon shows the ambivalence of this ideology toward science. It attacked science, as Mosse shows, even though in scientific and technological advances and the weaponry deriving from them lay Germany's hope of overcoming the numerically and economically more powerful Allies. This ambivalence also pertains to the rocket, which simultaneously attracts the Germans for mystical, sexual, and military reasons and yet repels them because of its destructiveness. This ideology appears in German folk literature in several ways in addition to the fearsome significance that characters find in the folk tale of Hansel and Gretel, which recurs as a leitmotif in this novel. The synthetic folk culture of Zwölfkinder, an amusement park near Peenemünde, allows an escape deserved by the beleaguered Pökler, but it also resembles the escapist films that, Kracauer argues, made many Germans susceptible to Hitler.

Among the German creators of high literature the most important pre-twentieth-century one, Goethe, gives Pynchon a geographical coincidence similar to the proximity of the Mittelwerke to Luther's homeland. One scene in *Gravity's Rainbow* opens with "Slothrop and the apprentice witch Geli Tripping, standing up on top of the Brocken, the very plexus of German evil, twenty miles north by northwest of the Mittelwerke" (p. 329). Goethe sets the witches' sabbath of part one of *Faust* on the Brocken because that place has traditional associations with witchcraft. Joseph W. Slade remarks that Margherita Erdmann (earth person), as her name implies, is part of the Faust motif in this novel (*Thomas Pynchon*, p. 207). Pynchon's characters also resemble Goethe's portrait of Faust. Richard Poirier notes that in *Gravity's Rainbow* "history-making man is Faustian man. But while this book offers such Faustian types as a rocket genius named Captain Blicero and a Pavlovian behaviorist named Edward Pointsman, it is evident that they are slaves to the systems they think they master" ("Rocket Power," p. 59).

In *V.* the Maltese have dual natures, one part being Faustian. They are "aimed two ways at once: towards peace and simplicity on the one hand, towards an exhausted intellectual searching on the other" (p. 289). Thus, despite the many characters in *Gravity's Rainbow* whose intellectual (usually scientific) and political power make them Faustian in one sense of the term, Faust figures play an even more prominent role in *V.* Most of the characters in the latter book actually exhibit only one side of the dual Maltese character; they are either Faustians or anti-Faustians. Moreover, this duality explains the book's structure. A nonintellectual search for love—mature love in the case of Paola and a few others, immature in the case of the Whole Sick Crew—manifests the anti-

Faustian sensibility, while Stencil's search for V. and the machinations of similar characters manifest the Faustian sensibility.

Pynchon also alludes to German values that can be attributed to the degradation of German romanticism. His juxtaposition in all three novels, especially in *V.*, of the desire on the one hand for love and simple pleasures and on the other hand for complex intellectual pursuits echoes the contrast between the two parts of *Faust*, the primary document of German romanticism. In the first part the natural Gretchen, a typical romantic heroine, satisfies Faust's simple needs, whereas in the second part the allegorical figure of Helen, an ideal woman of the classical era, satisfies Faust's complex intellectual needs. Goethe, of course, by combining the two parts, united the two sensibilities, and he created another synthesis by having German romanticism in the person of Faust mate with Greek classicism in the person of Helen to produce his human ideal: the Byronic Euphorion. Many decades later, the Goethean syntheses forgotten, enervated forms of romanticism helped prepare the climate for Hitler. Love of nature, for example, degenerated into the mysticism and chauvinism about German landscape that many German films and the characters in the scene on the Brocken in *Gravity's Rainbow* exhibit. In no way do Goethe or the other romantics deserve blame for these later transformations. Pynchon merely describes unobtrusively and implicitly, as he sketches in part of German cultural history, the degeneration of romantic values.[1]

Pynchon owes only a small debt to twentieth-century German writers, except to Rilke. Hermann Hesse plays a minor role in *Gravity's Rainbow*, sharing guilt with German mass culture for the mysticism that facilitated Hitler's ascent. The narrator bluntly points out Hesse's effects when he calls Kurt Mondaugen "one of these German mystics who grew up reading Hesse, Stefan George, and Richard Wilhelm, ready to accept Hitler on the basis of Demian-metaphysics, he seemed to look at fuel and oxidizer as paired opposites" (p. 403). Here Pynchon also suggests another explanation besides cybernetics for fascination with opposites. Other major twentieth-century German writers have not influenced Pynchon in any obvious way, although he resembles Kafka in tone, in his suggestion of vague, impending doom and in the multiple meanings one can attach to his symbols.

"The most important cultural figure in *Gravity's Rainbow*," as Richard Locke claims, is Rainer Maria Rilke (p. 2). Information about Rilke is indispensable for a full understanding of this novel. Rilke's early novel *The Notebooks of Malte Laurids Brigge*, although less important to Pynchon than his later poetry, opens in a way strikingly similar to the opening of *Gravity's Rainbow*. Rilke begins by describing an urban landscape full of objects with morbid connotations; a few pages later he mentions the experiences that induce the narrator to notice these images: the deaths of his father, mother, and grandfather, his viewing of a ghost, and his own illness. Both writers also describe in their first few pages shattered objects and a woman's scream. Thus, Rilke is another source for this section of Pynchon's novel. Malte himself exhibits many symptoms, but the most seriously paranoid character is his grandmother, who "carried with her the small, fine, silver sieve, through which she filtered everything she drank."[2]

Because Pynchon occasionally quotes from Rilke's later poetry, one can more easily establish a case for its influence on him. Locke analyzes the influence of only the *Duino Elegies*, but he makes several important discoveries. For instance, he quotes the beginning lines of the *Elegies*, including the prominent scream, and points out that "these lines are hideously amplified in the first words of Pynchon's novel" (p. 2). A similar echo, Locke also writes, occurs in the endings of the two books. He points out Rilke's portent of rebirth in the rising and falling imagery there. In contrast, the rocket falls at the novel's end, bringing death, not rebirth. Locke finds a Rilkean source for a recurring phenomenon, which is also explicable in psychological terms or as a borrowing from Lang's *Nibelungen*, when he calls the rocket's noise "a scream of sado-masochistic orgasm, a coming together in death, and this too is an echo and development of the exalted and deathly imagery of Rilke's poem" (p. 2). J. B. Leishman and Stephen Spender expand on Rilke's Liebestod sensibility and quote a letter in which he writes: "Only from the side of death, I believe, is it possible to do justice to love."[3]

One can trace the influences of the *Elegies* further than Locke does in his brief review. Even its dedication is relevant to Pynchon: "The property of Princess Marie von Thurn and Taxis-Hohenlohe." While he wrote the *Elegies* Rilke lived in the princess's castle in Duino. Her ancestors owned the postal monopoly mentioned in *The Crying of Lot 49*. Two possibilities can explain this relationship between the two writers. Pynchon may very early have been interested enough in Rilke to do research on the princess, thereby discovering the seed from which grew *The Crying of Lot 49*, or he may have become interested in Rilke only while he was writing *Gravity's Rainbow*, in which case the dedication's relevance to the earlier novel is the kind of coincidence that highly allusive writers produce most often.

Three times Pynchon quotes from the tenth elegy, in addition to the echo of it that Locke finds on the novel's last page. Rilke appeals to Weissmann more than to any other character:

> *Und nicht einmal sein Schritt klingt aus dem tonlosen Los.* . . . . Of all Rilke's poetry it's this Tenth Elegy he most loves, can feel the bitter lager of Yearning begin to prickle behind eyes and sinuses at remembering any passage of . . . the newly-dead youth, embracing his Lament, his last link, leaving now even her marginally human touch forever, climbing all alone, terminally alone, up and up into the mountains of primal Pain, with the wildly alien constellations overhead. . . . *And not once does his step ring from the soundless Destiny.* (p. 98)

While describing the specter visible to some over Lübeck and the Brocken, the narrator quotes *"O, wie spurlos zerträte ein Engel den Trostmarkt"* (p. 341). A few sentences later Pynchon cites the tenth elegy and translates part of the line he had quoted, expanding it to describe an event in Tchitcherine's past: "coming to trample spoorless the white marketplace of his own exile" (p. 341). Late in the book the narrator announces that "there is a mean poem about the Leid-Stadt, by a German man named Mr. Rilke" (p. 644). This remark refers to a passage a few lines earlier in the tenth elegy: "Freilich, wehe, wie fremd sind die Gassen der Leid-Stadt" ("Strange, though, alas! are the streets of the City of Pain") (pp. 78–79). In this elegy Rilke describes a traveler's progress through an allegorical setting. In these passages Pynchon borrows imagery from Rilke; in fact, he includes echoes of Rilke's elegy so often throughout this novel that it sometimes seems like an expanded version of that poem. Pynchon, however, uses these images for very different purposes. Rilke's screaming angel represents the ideal humanity that lies beyond mankind's reach; Pynchon's angel is the murderous rocket. In the elegy Rilke reconciles the lament and exultation that alternate in his last two books of poetry and ends this series of elegies by citing the rebirth that Locke mentions; Pynchon ends by describing an apocalypse during which the villains are destroyed.

The ninth elegy also figures prominently in *Gravity's Rainbow*. Weissmann finds in it the name he gives to his Herero double, Enzian. In the poem the name refers to an Alpine plant of blue and gold, the "Nordic colors" (p. 101). Pynchon claims that in this elegy the Enzian resembles a pure word, but Rilke actually writes about the word "Enzian" and about a traveler who brings back from a mountain only this word and nothing palpable such as dirt. A comment on the difficulty of finding words to express things forms this reference's context. Later Pynchon attributes a brief quotation to Rilke but does not mention that it comes from the ninth elegy. He gives only an English translation, not the original: "once, only once" (p. 413). The passage in Rilke describes an event that will happen only once yet cannot be canceled, but Pynchon contrasts this meaning with the cyclical conception of history symbolized by the benzene ring.

Gravity's Rainbow also resembles two general characteristics of the elegies. Leishman and Spender quote a letter in which Rilke writes that an intellectual's proper task after World War I is "to prepare in men's hearts the way for those gentle, mysterious, trembling transformations, from which alone the understandings and harmonies of a serener future will proceed" (p. 14). Pynchon's novel, which takes place during the last phase of World War II and a brief period afterward, also conveys a postwar sensibility. He, however, has much less hope than Rilke that he can make improvements. One can also learn indirectly about Pynchon from Leishman and Spender's description of Rilke's settings: "In reading the *Elegies*, we continually find ourselves in a kind of visionary landscape, where things are both familiar and unfamiliar, and where the distinction between inner and outer seems to have been abolished, or transcended" (p. 16). This quality in Pynchon and Rilke may derive from German Expressionistic painting.

Pynchon also borrows from Rilke's *Sonnets to Orpheus*, which, like the *Duino Elegies*, appeared in 1922. He quotes one passage from it without mentioning his source except to say it is Rilke:

> "Want the Change," Rilke said, "O be inspired by the Flame!" To laurel, to nightingale, to wind . . . *wanting* it, to be taken, to embrace, to fall toward the flame growing to fill all the senses and . . . not to love because it was no longer possible to act . . . but to be helplessly in a condition of love. . . .
>
> But not Katje: no mothlike plunge. He [Weissmann] must conclude that secretly she fears the Change. (p. 97)

Pynchon quotes here from the twelfth sonnet and then includes themes and images from this sonnet sequence. Another partially documented reference to one of the sonnets occurs much later:

> Like that Rilke prophesied,
>
>> And then Earthliness forget you,
>> To the stilled Earth say: I flow.
>> To the rushing water speak: I am. (p. 622)

This passage is part of the description of Slothrop finding the harmonica that long before he had lost down a toilet in Boston. In the context of the harmonica's reappearance the quotation is comic. In the original, however, this passage constitutes Rilke's final affirmation in the last stanza of his last sonnet. The contrast between Rilke's meaning and Pynchon's dramatizes the difference between their sensibilities.

More generally, screaming echoes throughout the sonnets. The opening of sonnet number twenty-six is typical:

> How the cry of a bird can stir us . . .
> Any once created crying,
> But even children, at play in the open,
> Cry past real cries.[4]

A more accurate translation of the German verb *schreien*—"to scream," not "to cry"—shows more clearly the similarity between Rilke and Pynchon. They both also allude to the myth of Orpheus, whom Slothrop resembles, a poet-lover wandering through an infernal landscape looking for a beloved. Slothrop, however, never finds a real love and makes only failing gestures of affection. These allusions thus have considerable importance in *Gravity's Rainbow*, though a little less than nonliterary allusions.

At the next level, however, where Pynchon shows the ways that various disciplines organize information, literature is more significant than the other disciplines. He continually demonstrates that a sophisticated work of literature does not communicate a predetermined nonliterary meaning from its beginning throughout its entire length. Rather, he suggests, it creates and conveys meaning gradually. One of the pronouncements in Robbe-Grillet's "New Novel, New Man" applies also to this strategy of Pynchon's: "The New Novel does not propose a ready-made signification."[5] To explain this point he adds that "the modern novel . . . is an exploration, but an exploration which itself creates its own significations, as it proceeds" (p. 141).

In the ending of *The Crying of Lot 49* Pynchon implies that his meaning emerges gradually. Oedipa goes to a stamp auction, hoping to learn the secret of the Tristero, because that postal system issued the stamps in the auction's lot 49. The novel, however, ends abruptly with Oedipa waiting. The last sentence, "Oedipa settled back, to await the crying of lot 49," does not divulge the answer to her problem (p. 138). In other words, Pynchon does not include the solution; the text fails her by ending at the crucial moment. Similarly, Oedipa's best evidence about the Tristero is *The Courier's Tragedy*, but its text fails her at the crucial time also, because she cannot choose from among the variants of the most important line. The absence of a solution underscores the novel's dependence on the riddle of the Tristero. Pynchon could have ended the book at any place by answering the riddle. His failure to do so makes the book in a sense openended, which in turn indicates that its meaning emerges gradually rather than being present from the beginning.

Second, the appearance of the eccentric title only in the final five words reveals something more about this novel. One might italicize those last five words, producing the novel's title and thereby discovering that the novel itself answers Oedipa's question. In other words, her search for meaning moves forward simultaneously with the book's creation of meaning, and the two movements end at exactly the same point. The gradually emerging meaning becomes complete only at the end. The actual creation of the book is thus a vital part of the book's meaning.

A comparison may explain this relation between Oedipa's search and Pynchon's writing. In "Dunyaziad" John Barth several times announces that "the key to the treasure is the treasure," making the same point that Pynchon implicitly makes in his ending. Barth bases his novella on a search, as Pynchon does, and then makes clear with his last words, as Pynchon does, that this search furnishes a means to produce a story. Moreover, with the last words of the book, *Chimera*, in which "Dunyaziad" appears, Barth produces the same effect that Pynchon produces with the last words of *The Crying of Lot 49*. The last words of Barth's book are "it's no *Bellerophoniad*. It's a."[6] The incomplete sentence makes this book even more clearly openended than Pynchon's. Barth's context, however, reveals the word that will correctly complete the sentence. The character who speaks those words simultaneously turns into a work of fiction, so the missing word is *Chimera*, the work of fiction that ends right there. Adding this word without italics would make this ending the exact equivalent of Pynchon's ending. Barth's book is indeed a chimera: a mysterious thing composed of three parts. Both endings produce the same effect; they suddenly reveal that the answer pursued throughout the book is the book itself. Such an ending also invites a reader to begin the book again. Pynchon makes this final point also with the last words of *Gravity's Rainbow*: "Now everybody."

Finally, the ending of *The Crying of Lot 49* puts the novel's spotlight on its author by showing that ultimately he is the source of all the information in the book. Pynchon reveals his hand in another way in this final scene, hinting that he has created all the previous effects in the book. The philatelist on whom Oedipa depends for technical information about stamps has learned about a "book bidder" for the stamps that may answer the riddle of the Tristero. A "book bidder" submits his bid anonymously beforehand rather than openly during the auction. That is, this anonymous bidder may buy the stamps and thus the vital answer and yet never reveal his identity. On a symbolic level, this bidder already controls the stamps and the answer. He is the book writer: Pynchon.

In summary, the process of creating this novel, and Pynchon's other two novels as well, is extremely significant. Pynchon continually calls attention to this process. The individual meanings matter as they emerge and then give way to other individual meanings. As demonstrated earlier, Pynchon's style, too, creates the sense of process, of the continuous production of new meaning. To put it another way, Pynchon works self-reflectively, attending to his creating as he creates. This creation constitutes the final pulling together of these novels' pieces. No nonliterary meaning unites these pieces. This is not to say that Pynchon's works are totally self-reflective, merely literature about literature, and thus sterile and meaningless. Rather, as Edward Mendelson claims, Pynchon contrasts vividly with the literary modernists who have brought literature to this blank wall.[7] Pynchon has avoided that self-reflectiveness partly by acknowledging the validity of nonliterary disciplines, even though he also points out their shortcomings. Lawrence Wolfley cites this deference: "More successfully than anyone else to date, he has assimilated into an essentially novelistic sensibility the pertinence of those powerful and antiliterary modes and tendencies that threaten to swamp a large part of the humanistic tradition" (p. 874).

As Pynchon tries to prevent a reader from reducing his books to nonliterary meanings or to compilations of data, he shows that literature, more than other forms of discourse, depends on certain methods of unification. For example, he unifies his works, in the absence of an imposed nonliterary meaning, by putting his materials together in patterns. Like many of his characters, he is fascinated by patterns; they try to discover them and he of course creates them. The paranoid motif in his work relates in this way to the literary motif, and he takes advantage of the pun on "plot." Writing about the patterns of double "S's" in *Gravity's Rainbow*, Richard Poirier remarks, "This kind of patterning has become a tiresome game, and in Pynchon it is, when blatant, usually the object of high spoofing, a symptom of mechanical paranoia" ("Rocket Power," p. 63). Poirier confuses, I think, psychological and literary patterns. True, patterns appear very frequently in Pynchon's work, but he needs them to assemble his literary fiction. The double "S's," for example, bring together the mathematical concept of the double integral, the Nazi SS insignia, and the shape of the Mittelwerke's tunnels. Pynchon thus tentatively offers scientific and mathematical data to explain the fascination of some Germans with the rocket and the ss. Such an explanation would do more than amuse the characters who try to grasp the rocket's secrets. Furthermore, it clarifies the psychological and cultural roots of Nazism.

Countless examples in Pynchon's work show his subtle pattern making. One example in *Gravity's Rainbow* relates one chapter to the next. In the first scene Slothrop spends the late morning and early afternoon "studying Professors Schiller on regenerative cooling, Wagner on combustion equations, Pauer and Beck on exhaust gases and burning efficiency" (p. 224). That night, in bed with Katje, he snuffs the candle without wetting his fingers and burns himself, so she kisses his fingers but cannot prevent blisters from forming. He awakens after she has gone and tries to reconstruct her departure: "She must have sat, smoking, watching him while he slept" (p. 226). The chapter ends as he smokes the unfinished cigarette she left behind. The next chapter begins by quoting Pavlov's lecture about the propensity of old people to focus on one stimulus and to exclude others. Pointsman's poem on this trait follows. The voice in this poem, that of an old person, disregards the other things in a room and attends to a flower:

Their spirits,
Or memories I kept of where they were,
Are canceled, for this moment, by the flame:

The metaphor for the flower, a flame, represents the most important actions of the previous chapter: Slothrop's studying combustion phenomena related to the rocket, his reckless snuffing of the candle, Katje's smoking, and his finishing her cigarette the next morning. The flame imagery connects these details to the rocket, as Pynchon shows in the list of Slothrop's study topics, and therefore ties both these scenes to the novel's most important symbol. The image of the flame also recurs in Rilke's poetry, the major literary influence on *Gravity's Rainbow*. A number of strands thus form a neat little pattern and are woven into the figure in the book's huge carpet.

An example of patterns within a chapter occurs later. Thanatz has been trying to be hit by lightning ever since he read a pamphlet about Benjamin Franklin. Pynchon contrasts ordinary people with those who either literally or metaphorically have been struck by lightning. The lives of ordinary people can be graphed by means of regular sine curves, but the lives of those who have been struck by lightning have at the points of impact cusps, points at which infinite change occurs. Then he imagines a secret society of the lightning-struck, including "handshakes with sharp cusp-flicks of fingernails" and a magazine called *A Nickel Saved* (p. 664). Several references to Franklin, lightning, and cusps tie together this scene. One can find countless other patterns in Pynchon's novels and short stories, but these two suffice to demonstrate how his imagination creates patterns and how these patterns are too significant to be either spoofs or symptoms of paranoia.

Pynchon's perpetual concern with language is a second unifying force in his work. From "Entropy" through *Gravity's Rainbow* he has documented the trouble that people have when they cannot articulate or communicate with others. Some critics have covered this subject. Tony Tanner argues convincingly that in *V.* "language has suffered an incurable decline" (p. 160). Anne Mangel finds the same motif in Pynchon's second novel: "The redundancy, irrelevance, ambiguity, and sheer waste involved in language glare from every page of *The Crying of Lot 49*" (pp. 206-7). She, too, offers a sufficient number of examples, although I do not think that language deserves the blame. These flaws do not inhere in it, otherwise Pynchon could not use it so effectively. Rather, his characters create the problems themselves by their slovenly use of language.

In *Gravity's Rainbow* the characters use language more expertly. Instead of struggling with it, they theorize about it. At times language seems almost magical, and the characters resemble Adam and Eve naming the things around them and marveling at the conjunction of thing and sound. At one point " 'Raketemensche!' screams Säure, grabbing the helmet and unscrewing the horns off of it. Names by themselves may be empty, but the *act of naming. . . .*" (p. 366). The ellipsis is in the text, signifying that Säure's amazement prevents him from continuing to speak. The characters in this novel will go to great lengths to understand language because they have great faith in its efficacy. Some of them gather at a conference and argue heatedly and comically about very technical and trivial issues in phonetics. In most cases, however, their concern is not misplaced, for linguistic facility repeatedly allows them to solve problems. One apparently trivial example joins with an episode in *The Crying of Lot 49* to make a crucial point. Slothrop has much difficulty mastering German circuit diagrams, because he thinks that the symbol for a resistor looks like an actual coil and vice versa. Sir Stephen Dodson-Truck, however, explains: "That coil symbol there happens to be very like the Old Norse rune for "S," *sol*, which means "sun." The Old High German name for it is *sigil'* " (p. 206). That is, one energy source represents another, but to realize this and to understand the circuit diagram fully one needs considerable knowledge of languages. In *Gravity's Rainbow* Pynchon himself demonstrates at least some knowledge of many languages, including such exotic ones as Herero. Early in *The Crying of Lot 49* Oedipa's confusion begins when she sees in both a city and a circuit only hidden meaning, failure to communicate. Critics have pounced on this passage, sometimes using it as evidence of Pynchon's alleged absurdism. Considered with the passage in *Gravity's Rainbow* about the circuit, however, it suggests that linguistic mastery will solve the puzzle of circuits and other puzzles as well.

As Pynchon shows how writers create literature he also shows how literature relates to reality. He accomplishes this most effectively by announcing his artifice and using works within works to mix the real and the fictive. As to the former technique, many of his characters have theatrical traits and perform roles rather than express a consistent self. In his fiction "humans are akin to props in a cruel and dehumanizing play by author or authors unknown," as Tony Tanner claims, and "(of course Pynchon is aware of the additional irony that these characters are also caught up in a play arranged by *him*—the affliction of his characters is the condition of his form)" (p. 160). Tanner describes the powerlessness of the characters so that one can see its roots in their fictiveness. He also shows still another way in which Pynchon directs his reader's attention to the author. The theatricality of the characters becomes undeniable in the play within *The Crying of Lot 49*. After a while this play begins to dominate the participants' personalities, and the director, worried that his life will become fictive in the same way, drowns himself. The play also gives Oedipa important information about the Tristero. This mingling of the "real" and the "fictive" in a work of literature causes one to wonder whether the two can be separated.

Pynchon uses another method to mix levels of reality within his works and thereby further elucidates the nature of literature. As part of his own literary fiction he describes characters trying to construct their own fictions. At least one character's effort to do this constitutes a vital part of each of Pynchon's novels. Herbert Stencil, like his father, Sidney, devotes most of his energy to trying to solve the mysteries of V. Oedipa Maas tries to combine pieces of data to explain the Tristero. In *Gravity's Rainbow* Slothrop particularly and also some other characters try to understand the German rocket both as a technological product and as a symbol. Although Slothrop makes the most progress, none of the characters succeeds to any great extent.

The main narrators, who have no identity or qualities, try to fit all the pieces together. They operate in unusual ways, interrupting the narrative to speculate on the characters' thoughts and then putting these imagined thoughts into a context. A quotation about metaphor typifies this mode of narration. In *V.* Fausto, presenting his confessions, comments: "Manhood on Malta thus became increasingly defined in terms of rockhood. This had its dangers for Fausto. Living as he does much of the time in a world of metaphor, the poet is always acutely conscious that metaphor has no value apart from its function" (p. 305). In this passage Pynchon characteristically and importantly shifts from "Fausto" to "the poet." The opinions that follow thus could be Fausto's by implication or they could be those of a typical poet. Most likely they belong to Fausto, in his role as narrator of his confessions, as he tries to understand one of his former personalities and to determine how typical of poets these opinions are. That is, Fausto arrives at the opinions by making a fiction, a theory about poets. The narrators make more successful fictions than do the questing characters because they have both more information—they gather it from other characters as well—and more skill in creating fictions. Their dependence on speculation, illustrated in this quotation, suggests, however, that their fictions do not fully succeed. Above them, in turn, stands Pynchon, the ultimate fictionmaker.

In one sense, but not in the usual sense, readers have been participating in *Gravity's Rainbow* all the way through it. Very likely they will not empathize with the characters, who are not totally believable or similar to themselves. Nor, for example, will they imagine themselves on a rocket hunt and thus become absorbed in the plot's surface aspects. Instead, like many other powerful novels, *Gravity's Rainbow* places its reader in the same quandary that the main character faces. Like Slothrop and the narrator, the reader must organize a multitude of data. A reader thereby gets a sense of fiction making even if he does not realize the importance to Pynchon's novel of this activity.

A thorough analysis of the literary fictions in some of Pynchon's works will clarify these generalizations. It makes most sense to begin with a short story. Critics have discussed "Entropy" at some length, whereas they have neglected another fine story, "Low-lands," which is a suitable object for this kind of attention. To show how a literary fiction operates, one needs to approach this story differently from the usual analysis. Rather than focus directly on the elements of fiction, I will evoke them only indirectly by elucidating the story's nonliterary and literary fictions. Suffice it to say that the elements of fiction in "Low-lands" function as they do in all Pynchon's stories and novels: to demonstrate the necessity of fictions. Because a literary fiction is not guided from the story's beginning to its end by a few ideas, a critic pursuing this method should not begin by seeking literary statements of nonliterary ideas. On the other hand, my definition of a literary fiction implies a method of analysis and a list of features a critic who uses it must notice. First, because a literary fiction reflects on itself, a critic needs to determine the statements, implicit as well as explicit, that the author makes about constructing fictions. Second, a literary fiction creates its order by forming patterns; therefore, a critic needs to observe the patterns in the work. Third, because a literary fiction assimilates non-literary fictions, a critic should understand how they are interrelated.

In "Low-lands" self-reflection appears in the stories within the story, as is often the case in literary fictions. At the garbage dump Pig Bodine, Flange, and Bolingbroke each tell a story to the others and to Rocco. The stories themselves and their context reveal several theories about the nature of storytelling. For example, a reader can deduce several reasons for telling stories. First, these three characters tell them to pass the time because none of the four men knows all three of the others, three of them have suddenly arrived at a strange place, and they have little to do. Second, they try to amuse each other. Pig's story, if one can avoid moralizing about it, contains some physical humor, and Flange's story, although macabre, has amusing aspects. The reversal in Bolingbroke's story, the sudden friendship of captain and mutineer, is a traditional comic device. Third, the storytellers glorify some of their own positive character traits. Pig shows his unfettered spirit and physical bravery, Flange his cleverness, and Bolingbroke his composure despite the outrageous behavior of others. The rest of the short story demonstrates that they do indeed possess these characteristics, although Flange's wife gives other names to the trait that Pig considers independence. Flange broods sensitively on his difficulties and wins verbal battles with his wife, even though she dominates him in practical terms. Bolingbroke stoically endures the gypsies and the three intruders into his domain.

Finally, they tell the stories to understand themselves, and because they remain unaware of this purpose they inadvertently reveal negative personality traits. Pig validates the claim of Flange's wife that he resembles a wild animal. Flange reveals his marital problems. His story of putting a woman's corpse into a friend's bed and then asking through the door whether he has a woman in his room is an analogy to Flange's unhappy marriage because he considers his wife to be figuratively dead. Bolingbroke unwittingly shows his wariness about authority, which is often justifiable. For example, at the beginning of his story he tries to justify the seizure of the ship by mentioning that it is registered in Panama, which may indicate that its owners are trying to conceal its activities. He immediately apologizes for including this detail, as if he senses the inadequacy of this self-defense and the personal quality that prompted it. His failure to tell anyone about the gypsies lest he himself be suspected reveals the same kind of uneasiness.

Only certain kinds of patterns help to unify the literary fiction: the patterns formed by details that can be attributed directly to the author, such as the characters' names, the most basic features of the plot and setting, and the images that derive from these other basic features. Details that the narrator or the characters add as part of their own attempts to make fictions are not included. According to these terms two recurring images and a concept suggested by a name and part of the setting qualify. One of these images, the tunnels, occurs unobtrusively in the description of the tunnels in the garbage dump. The other image, the sea, appears in Pig's and Bolingbroke's stories, in Flange's comparison of it to a solid block, in his house's location on Long Island Sound, in the Scottish ballad that furnishes the story's title, in Flange's and Pig's occupation as sailors, and in the story's final words: "Whitecaps danced across her eyes; sea creatures, he knew, would be cruising about in the submarine green of her heart" (p. 108). The concept of waste that plays such an important role in Pynchon's writing from this story onward is expressed here by setting part of the story in a dump. Later, as he does in the SHROUD scene in *V.* Pynchon visualizes humans turning into objects as part of the effects of entropy, or increasing waste. These patterns unify this story and communicate meaning.

One must classify the nonliterary fictions in order to determine the efficacy of the various kinds. Classification according to the fiction's creator does not work well, because Pynchon quickly discredits all the creators except himself, thereby thwarting all efforts to make fine distinctions by means of this classification about the worth of various kinds of nonliterary fictions. A discussion of this discrediting will, however, also reveal Pynchon's method of operation. To follow this line of analysis one needs first to identify the fictions because not everything in the story qualifies. To find them one looks for efforts to arrange details into a comprehensible pattern in order to make sense of something. Raw details do not qualify, nor do unexamined actions. One of the narrator's fictions, the assertion that the former owner of Flange's house found it convenient to smuggle liquor during Prohibition because he lived on the north shore of Long Island Sound, constitutes a sensible attempt to explain actions by means of geographical influences. Next, however, the narrator tries to understand the house by means of two historical fictions, calling the minister's attitude romantic but also making two analogies between the house and prehistoric objects: a tumulus (an ancient burial mound) and the color of prehistoric beasts. The narrator's confusion of this historical fiction, shown by his likening the house to objects existing in two widely separated eras, shows that the narrator's fictions will not always work.

The characters also find it difficult to form workable fictions. Pig Bodine, Rocco, Bolingbroke, and Flange's wife do not create fictions but merely take things as they come. They do have characteristic ways of reacting, such as Pig's hedonism and Mrs. Flange's moralism and practicality, but they do not reflect enough to order things. Nerissa has one fiction, an occult one. Because she believes a fortune-teller's prediction that she will marry a blond Anglo, she tries to lure Flange away from Bolingbroke's cabin despite his dark hair. The story ends without making it clear whether or not they will marry, but her ignoring of, or misconception about, his hair makes her fiction questionable. Flange and his psychiatrist accept Freudian fictions, but Flange convincingly calls the psychiatrist crazy. Although none of these characters creates a fiction or fictions that *always* work, sometimes they do succeed.

Another way of classifying, by field of knowledge, cogently reveals the literary fiction's evaluation of nonliterary fictions. The narrator's twofold explanation of the minister's house makes historical fictions suspect. Artistic fictions also yield mixed results. The Noel Coward song that Flange cites misrepresents his marriage, but the ballad about the low-lands relates to the sea imagery throughout the story, and the Spanish galleon that captures the other ship may symbolize either Nerissa or Diaz, the Mexican psychiatrist (the former being much more likely). Both capture Flange for his benefit; the psychiatrist helps by proposing the metaphor that the sea is a woman, which is supported by the sea imagery. Flange's comparison of his wife to a Mondrian painting, although interesting, explains little. Pynchon names the dump's attendant Bolingbroke, but this hesitant man does not resemble Shakespeare's portrait of that person. Oddly, then, literary history does not form an effective fiction in this story.

Four other kinds of fiction appear only once each, so even those that work do not explain enough to be very valuable. Flange's belief in fate avoids evaluation because although nothing in the story disproves this interpretation, neither does anything support it. The mathematical fiction in which he conceives of

Bolingbroke's house as the center and bottom of a spiral helps him orient himself spatially but otherwise has no value. His citation of Heisenberg's Principle of Indeterminacy to justify remaining passive rather than seeking knowledge runs counter to the story's ending, in which the sea imagery climaxes in the comparison of Nerissa to the sea. This pattern and metaphor have positive connotations, and Flange finds Nerissa by actively seeking the source of the voice that calls him. Nerissa's occult fiction, her belief in the fortune-teller's prediction, although it does not accord with Flange's hair color, does lead to their meeting. This fiction's effect more than balances its misrepresentation.

Geographical and psychological fictions are more revealing than any of the others. The narrator's belief that the geography of Long Island's northern shore caused its residents to be bootleggers during Prohibition makes sense in the light of Pynchon's symbolic use of two geographical features: the sea and the tunnels. The image of Nerissa's womb-like cave, where he feels comfortable, validates Flange's two psychological fictions based on the theory that some people desire to return to the womb. When geography and psychology combine in the metaphor of the sea as woman, an even more useful fiction results. Flange's idea that the sea has solidity and will support people is another hybrid. Diaz calls this idea evidence of a Messiah complex, an interpretation that is not supported by anything in the story. Combined with the metaphor of the sea as woman and with the optimism surrounding his and Nerissa's meeting, Flange's idea means that their relationship will be satisfying.

In summary, two of the most important themes in "Lowlands" are the creation and the validity of fictions. Starting from this assumption a reader can clarify all the important details of the story and avoid oversimplifying it. For example, the presence of the psychiatrist and some of the imagery could easily tempt the reader to consider this story a Freudian parable, an assumption that ignores much of its meaning. Pynchon does use Freudian ideas, but his main purpose is to analyze fictions. A reader who understands that analysis will better understand one method that people often use to make sense of the world.

Although the length of Pynchon's novels makes it difficult to analyze their fictions, one can do so, at least to the extent of pointing out the salient features. The same method of analysis is useful for both short stories and novels, but for novels one needs to make finer distinctions and to work with more material. By the same token, in his novels Pynchon has made more subtle and important fictions than in his short stories, and elucidating them, particularly the one in *Gravity's Rainbow*, will climax this study.

The first point at which a finer distinction is necessary concerns the first object of study in an analysis of fictions: the role of stories within the main story. The problem arises because a novelist can create multiple narrators. Four times in *V.* a character interrupts the narrative voice and begins to tell part of the story. In two cases this is accomplished through the introduction of documents: Father Fairing's journal and Fausto Maijstral's confessions (p. 106 ff., p. 184 ff.). Because they are presented as parts of documents, these two stories have more apparent credibility than the other two. In fact, the status of the other two, the story of intrigue set in Egypt and the story of Kurt Mondaugen in German Southwest Africa, is quite questionable because of their narrator (pp. 52 ff., pp. 211 ff.). Herbert Stencil tells both, reconstructing the former from scanty information in a journal and revising the latter as he tells it to Eigenvalue. His tendency to "stencilize," to see everything according to his own preconceptions, demonstrates the personal element in fictions. In any case, these four examples should not be accepted as stories within stories because to be a valid candidate for this category a story should interrupt the main plot and be clearly separate from it, rather than merely the effect of a change of narrators. It also must be self-enclosed, reasonably unified, fairly brief, and narrative rather than discursive. The stories in "Low-lands" are classic examples of this technique.

In all of *V.* only one story, about the golden screw in someone's navel, fits these specifications (p. 30). Amusing to some, it does not amuse Profane, who, according to the narrator, tells it to himself. Nor, unlike the storytellers in "Low-lands," does he want to pass time, amuse others, or glorify himself. He tells the story because it explains things to himself. The narrator, perhaps too obviously, points out that the story's humor derives from the improbability that disassembly of a person will occur. This story, although unlikely, does warn about a danger that occasionally occurs in *V.* Thus, it explains something about human existence. The story, because of its emphasis on disassembly, also recalls entropy, one of Pynchon's favorite metaphors for human existence. The rest of this novel therefore validates Profane's story, despite his intellectual limitations and his story's broad humor.

Fiction, a larger category than the story within the story, has the same meaning here as it has had throughout this study, and one can easily find examples of fictions. The characters' most important fictions can simply be listed. Stencil, the most active fictionmaker, constructs two other fictions in addition to those about intrigue and about Mondaugen. He explains politics with the metaphor of the hothouse and the street (p. 400). More important, his fiction about V. dominates his life, and his efforts to piece it together provide much of the plot's impetus. In addition to his confessions, Fausto Maijstral propounds a theory of history, arguing that it can be graphed as a sine curve (p. 287). Other characters each create one fiction: Mafia Winsome's concept of Heroic Love, Eigenvalue's psychodontia, McClintic Sphere's cybernetic-like theory of opposites that leads him to advise "keep cool but care," Dnubietna's theory that history is a step-function, and the children of Malta's imaginative conception of the wheel of fortune. When these and the other fictions are arranged according to fields of knowledge, it will become clear that none of the characters has made a universally applicable fiction.

The shortcoming of the narrator's fictions, however, are immediately apparent. He forms three that depend on the theory that the world remains static. A scientific fiction describes a cosmic oscillation like the many instances in the book of yo-yoing (p. 26), he states a fiction based on the existence of external Jungian archetypes (p. 183), and he also recounts three scientific conceptions of humanity, which, although they are not identical and have gained acceptance in different centuries, all imply that a person can be reduced to a plaything of constant physical forces (p. 265). In contrast, he also predicates three of these fictions on a belief in the world's dynamism, specifically, on its constant deterioration. The first of them, his reference to the decadence that comes at the end of an age, implies a cyclical notion that a better time will follow. The other two dynamic fictions more bleakly allow for no renewal. One, the theory of entropy, predicts a universal loss of energy, except in a few scattered areas (p. 301), and the other conceives of history as moving inexorably toward greater destruction (p. 433). Thus, by proposing fictions based on contradictory premises the narrator discredits himself.

Next, one needs to discover the patterns that reveal fictions attributable to Pynchon. The characters' names give no clue because although many of them are significant, their importance varies greatly. The bare bones of the plot give a better clue. This plot has two strands: Stencil's search for V. and the search by other characters for more earthy satisfactions, especially love and lust. Seen in the light of fictionmaking, this bifurcation takes a new meaning. Stencil's search demonstrates the importance of fictions because it energizes the plot and also because Stencil cannot avoid making fictions. Fictionmaking is more than important to him, and to ruminative people in general; it is necessary. On the other hand, making fictions, by greatly complicating life, can preclude the simple pleasures described by the other strand of the plot. Thus Pynchon composes his plot to demonstrate the basic dilemma of the fictionmaker. Other elements of the basic plot— the frequent instances of inanimateness and oscillation—support scientific fictions. Three parts of this novel's setting—the tunnels, the street, and Malta—are symbols, but each has multiple meanings and thus none consistently illuminates the fictions. Nor does an important recurring image, mirrors, clarify; instead, it represents perverted action in general.

The next step, categorizing the fictions made by the characters and the narrator and then analyzing them according to the patterns Pynchon makes, reveals his evaluation of these fictions. The scientific ones explain things accurately but disturbingly. That is, many of the characters show themselves to be reducible to entities that are victimized by physical forces. All of the historical fictions make sense of some data but their multiplicity means that they overlap. The psychological fictions have little use. Psychodontia and Heroic Love illustrate, respectively, inanimateness and perverted love but little else. The Jungian theory of archetypes explains only those characters who obsessively continue to seek the same things. Because of the relatively minor importance of politics in this novel, the political fiction of the hothouse and the street explains little. Science, then, provides the most useful fictions in this novel.

The literary fiction that Pynchon creates in *The Crying of Lot 49* has a very different meaning from the ones in "Low-lands" and *V*. According to the definition given earlier, he does not include any stories within the main story. Instead, he includes a film and a play, cleverly connecting them by having *Cashiered* caricature *The Courier's Tragedy*, which in turn parodies Jacobean revenge tragedy. Oedipa tries to determine how the plots of both the film and the play will end. Her efforts to guess the film's ending are comic, but she studies the play seriously because she thinks that it will solve the Tristero's enigmas. In the film the enemy has a definite identity, whereas in the play it never becomes clear whether or not the enemy is part of a larger conspiracy. In summary, Pynchon develops much more fully the artistic fictions and shows that they can illuminate each other, even when they do not illuminate the real world.

Of the characters in this novel, Oedipa makes the most important fictions. She sees a hieroglyph in San Narciso's physical appearance, makes the intricate metaphor that links delirium tremens and time differential, and puts together a multitude of clues to arrive at her belief that the Tristero may actually exist. Dr. Hilarius gradually creates a paranoid fiction. Oedipa's husband believes that people who have voices that can be broken into the same components and who say the same words have the same identity. Fallopian, influenced by the paranoia of the Peter Pinguid Society, works on an historical fiction based on the theory that postal reform caused the Civil War.

The next two steps in an analysis of this novel's fictions produce strange results. Characters create all the important fictions; the narrator creates none. This unusual apportioning increases the Tristero's obscurity, for the reader receives no help from the narrator. Nor do the patterns that Pynchon creates offer much help. The names again have various kinds of associations, rather than forming a consistent pattern. The main pattern in the basic plot, the Tristero's apparent emergence at brief intervals, does not help to solve problems. Rather, it presents one of the novel's central problems: does the Tristero exist or not? The setting, California, provides an object for social commentary, but it does not clearly yield a symbolic meaning, as do the settings in *V.* and "Low-lands." Oedipa sees a hieroglyph in part of the setting, but its existence is not clear, nor is its meaning. As to the images, the tower in the painting helps to clarify the novel's action. Again, then, an artistic fiction casts light and this time that light shines on the novel's main action rather than on another artistic fiction within the novel. No recurring images have much importance, so another potential source of illumination produces nothing. The narrator's fictions and the patterns thus add to the enigmas of this novel rather than help to solve them.

Confusion begins to be dispelled, however, when one reaches the final stage of analysis and examines the types of fiction. In *The Crying of Lot 49*, as in *V.*, scientific fictions explain better than do other kinds. The crucial one, Oedipa's metaphor connecting delirium tremens and time differential offers the most important clue (pp. 95–96). As she makes this metaphor, she contemplates the nature of metaphor, thus creating the effects that Pynchon achieves in *V.* and "Low-lands" by including stories within stories. Metaphor, she claims, shields people from having to face life unmediated, for without it the decay of everything in time becomes painfully evident. By extension, a fiction—an intricate and greatly extended metaphor—constructs the same kind of barrier. In *V.* Pynchon considers the dangers of not making fictions, of confronting more reality than one can bear. The other scientific metaphors in this novel relate to this last point. Entropy explains decay as time passes, and Maxwell's Demon, by constructing a set of opposites, purports to escape decay. A metaphor about a computer also contains a set of opposites (p. 136). Most of the other types of fiction derive from a dualistic system, too: Hilarius's paranoia, Oedipa's notion of the Tristero and the official system, and Fallopian's conception of history as a war between two rival postal networks. Similarly, the Peter Pinguid Society makes a dualistic political fiction, and the

Scurvhamites make a dualistic religious fiction (pp. 31, 116). Up
to this point Pynchon suggests that people create fictions to avoid
a direct encounter with reality and that many of their fictions are
dualistic.

The painting of the tower, however, is more impressive (pp. 10-
11). It depicts women weaving a patterned tapestry that becomes
a world. From this painting Oedipa deduces ideas that help her to
understand her own problems, but this work of art also has other
properties. Pynchon has constructed a Chinese box system: a
tapestry inside a painting inside a novel. All of these boxes are
works of art and they illuminate both each other and finally the
nature of fictions. Moreover, no dualism limits these works of art,
nor do they replace or flee the world: like the painting and the
novel, "the tapestry was the world" (p. 10). David Crowart explains that, although she has a Pynchonesque name, Remedios
Varo is a real painter and she did paint *Bardando el Manto
Terrestre*[8].

In *Gravity's Rainbow* Pynchon continues his trend of
increasingly more profound analyses of fictions. In this novel he
includes only one story. The only other possible story, about
Morituri, does not qualify because it only switches narrators in
order to carry on the same plot line as the rest of the novel. The
only intercalated story, the account of Byron Bulb, resembles
Cashiered in *The Crying of Lot 49* because it describes a character
threatened by a force that certainly exists. Unlike that film, and
even though its hero is a light bulb, this story is not merely a
humorous caricature of the problem of a novel's main character.
Somehow Pynchon maintains seriousness and makes Byron a
paradigm of the alien in a hostile world.

At least a dozen of the characters in *Gravity's Rainbow* create
fictions. Even some madmen, such as the man who thinks he is
World War II, and some dead people, such as Walter Rathenau
and William Slothrop, make fictions. Most noticeably, the
characters in this novel make brief fictions—and usually only one
apiece—that, compared to the many fictions in the book, offer
little promise. Many of the characters construct fictions that
explain Slothrop's experiences, but he constructs fewer fictions
than does Oedipa. Pynchon makes it clear that she tries to

discover whether positing the existence of the Tristero will explain her experiences. In contrast, Slothrop interrupts his search for the rocket, and he often tries to understand its technology rather than any larger, metaphysical meaning it may have. He meditates less and forges on against confusion less resolutely than does Oedipa. In *Gravity's Rainbow*, then, fictions have even more value than in the earlier novels, but constructing them appears to be nearly impossible.

Like the characters, the narrator of *Gravity's Rainbow* makes many different kinds of brief fictions. In fact, he duplicates some of the characters' fictions. For example, Vanya gives a Marxist critique of history, attributing change to economic factors, and the narrator points out the great power of Shell and other international corporations (pp. 155, 251). Thus, Pynchon's tactic in this novel contrasts vividly to that of *The Crying of Lot 49*. In the earlier book he gives no criterion by which to evaluate the characters' fictions, whereas in the latter book the narrator supports many of the characters' fictions, which also makes evaluation difficult, because it seems to support contradictory interpretations. Pynchon also works his fictions more neatly into the texture of *Gravity's Rainbow* than in his first two novels. Some of these fictions, such as the history of the German film, lie hidden. As in the tapestry scene in *The Crying of Lot 49*, Pynchon includes in *Gravity's Rainbow* a parable about artistic fictions: the obscure episode of the Forlorn Four (pp. 675–81). Slothrop and three bad artists (bad in Pynchon's terms) comprise this group. Maximilian is too much the dandy, too dependent on style and vitality. Myrtle, the super-realist, allows a different kind of spectacular talent, the ability to duplicate real objects, to dominate and corrupt her. Marcel, the mechanical chess player, is Proust; he does "exquisite 19th-century brainwork" but has no live parts to redeem his plastic, mechanical nature, and he tediously elaborates his themes (p. 675). Here Pynchon pleads for humanly significant art that neither duplicates nor evades everyday reality but clarifies it.

Pynchon himself, despite the vast erudition in *Gravity's Rainbow*, has written a novel that meets the specifications he sets forth in this parable. This novel has a strong emotional impact, showing concern for confused, powerless people. It thereby resolves a dilemma implicit in *V.*: the need to make fictions yet to retain a chance of satisfying simpler needs, such as the need for love. W. T. Lhamon, Jr., responds to this quality of *Gravity's Rainbow*: "Reading [it] is a primary experience. I felt anguish about reading it alone, needed to touch the person next to me, as Pynchon urges throughout" (p. 28). Pynchon's humanity appears most obviously in the scene where Pökler slips his ring on the finger of a nearly dead woman. This silent acknowledgment of human solidarity is much more impressive than Sphere's unconvincing advice in *V.* or Oedipa's reaction to the drunk in *The Crying of Lot 49*, which is diluted by the dissertation on metaphors that follows. This quality helps justify the great energy necessary to understand the cerebral aspects of *Gravity's Rainbow*.

The patterns in this novel also support many kinds of fictions, certainly the ones that have been important throughout Pynchon's career. The rocket's profound meaning justifies many scientific fictions. He includes examples of historical repetition and evidence of both the importance of various eras and our era's movement toward apocalypse, and he implies the validity of other historical fictions. The many passages clarified by knowledge of films lend credence to this kind of fiction. The characters exhibit traits that reinforce various psychological fictions. In fact, when one weighs these patterns against the different types of fictions in the novel it becomes clear that the type of fiction matters less than the human needs that a fiction satisfies and the degree to which it can be integrated into a work of art.

In short, Pynchon's examination of this artistic medium has reached an important juncture. Throughout his career he has speculated on its nature and its relation to other media, thereby casting a coldly intellectual light on his work. In *Gravity's Rainbow*, however, he has both found the understanding he sought and discovered how to make his writing more humanly important. By culminating the first process and beginning the second, his most recent novel achieves the status of a major work. He now stands ready to create even more impressive books.

Conclusion

Pynchon's conception of the mission of literature is distinctive. With great skill he manipulates the traditional elements of fiction in order to reveal the inadequacy of realistic literary conventions and commonsense epistemologies, and he builds small new constructs, using information from nonliterary fields, borrowing especially from science, psychology, history, religion, and film. Finally, he gradually creates a complex literary fiction that incorporates, interrelates, and evaluates nonliterary information and ways of organizing it.

After Pynchon's accomplishments have been described, the merits of his work can be evaluated. Pynchon's youth—he was only thirty-five when he published *Gravity's Rainbow*—requires that any judgment be tentative, because he undoubtedly will write much more. He now has published a substantial body of material, however, and the appearance of a book as ambitious as *Gravity's Rainbow* makes this an appropriate time to take stock. Most of his short stories are significant mainly as they relate to his longer works; he even incorporates some of them into his novels. Among them, "Entropy" and "Low-lands" are the most impressive. Although the former has received more attention, the latter is also a fine work. His essay on Watts deserves more readers because it incisively, yet far from dispassionately, portrays that neighborhood. *V.* has deservedly drawn high praise and has done so not just as a promising first novel. The two plots could mesh a little more neatly but it, too, dramatizes important issues and integrates a good deal of knowledge into a novelistic form. Highly sophisticated critics and a literary underground looking for apocalyptic visions have taken up this book's cause, the former being more cognizant of Pynchon's real achievement. In a sense *The Crying of Lot 49* recapitulates themes and techniques already presented in *V.*, but it does so with no wasted motion. In it, Pynchon created a small jewel, a novel with considerable complexity yet unity of effect.

Gravity's Rainbow combines the virtues of his first two novels. Simply put, it is one of the masterpieces of the twentieth-century American novel. Edward Mendelson, for example, claims that "few books in this century have held so large a vision of the world in a structure so skillfully and elaborately conceived. This is certainly the most important novel to be published in English in the past thirty years" ("Pynchon's Gravity," p. 631). Only in the years to come, after more critical work, will readers be able to estimate more accurately its greatness. Even now, however, one can detect two apparently contradictory qualities in the book: Pynchon demonstrates great intellectual daring and erudition and at the same time maintains complete aesthetic control over his materials. A reader can understand this achievement either by repeated probing at a small part in order to see the texture's richness or by tracing the development of a technique, image, or theme through the 740 pages to see the control. Because of Pynchon's skills *Gravity's Rainbow* teaches us how to understand our world.

Always important, the lesson he teaches has now become indispensable. "The critical issue, given the perpetual assumption of crisis," writes Frank Kermode, "is no less than the justification of ideas of order."[1] Kermode cites earlier eras that cried out for order; surely ours, rent perpetually by traumas, cries as loudly as any. The "Protean men" that Robert Jay Lifton finds in so many places give evidence that disturbing changes are occurring.[2] Lifton's convincing argument that many people create for themselves a sequence of personalities, often juxtaposing vastly different ones, shows the need for fictions. That is, some people even make fictions out of themselves. If Pynchon has created a valid idea of order, he has done humanity a great service.

Pynchon also can guide other creators of prose narrative. The novel has not died, but its practitioners have driven it into a corner. There, boxed in, it has begun to examine itself. Such self-contemplation—novels about little except themselves—has gone on long enough. Fundamental theoretical problems still remain, but the task now should be to solve them while creating novels that also have other kinds of import. Pynchon's conception of literature as a fiction among other fictions offers a way to do this. It precludes abandoning the art of prose to non-novelistic or pseudo-novelistic pursuits, and it allows for both self-examination and use of other kinds of fiction.

Notes

Introduction

1. C.P. Snow, *The Two Cultures and the Scientific Revolution* (New York: Cambridge University Press, 1959), p. 8.
2. George Levine, "V-2," *Partisan Review*, 40 No. 3 (1973), 518.

Chapter One

1. *Gravity's Rainbow* (New York: The Viking Press, 1973), pp. 14 ff. For this novel and Pynchon's other two I will cite, with page numbers in parentheses, the paperback edition. The others are *V.* (New York: Bantam Books, 1964) and *The Crying of Lot 49* (New York: Bantam Books, 1967). The last two appeared a year after Lippincott published the hardbound editions. *Gravity's Rainbow* appeared simultaneously in paper and hardbound.
2. George Levine, "Risking the Moment: Anarchy and Possibility in Pynchon's Fiction," ed. George Levine and David Leverenz, *Mindful Pleasures: Essays on Thomas Pynchon* (Boston: Little, Brown and Company, 1976), p. 113.
3. "Under the Rose," *The Noble Savage*, 3 (Spring 1961), 223-51.
4. Scott Simmon, *"Gravity's Rainbow* Described," *Critique*, 16, No. 2 (1974), 63.
5. Richard Locke, *"Gravity's Rainbow," New York Times Book Review*, 11 March 1973, p. 14.

6. Tony Tanner, *City of Words* (New York: Harper and Row, 1971), p. 156.

7. David K. Kirby, "Two Modern Versions of the Quest," *Southern Humanities Review*, 5, No. 4 (Fall 1971), 392.

8. Joseph W. Slade, *Thomas Pynchon* (New York: Warner Paperback Library, 1974), p. 174.

9. Richard Poirier, "The Importance of Thomas Pynchon," *Twentieth Century Literature*, 21, No. 2 (May 1975), 156-57.

10. W. T. Lhamon, Jr., "The Most Irresponsible Bastard," *New Republic*, 168, No. 15 (14 April 1973), 24.

11. "The Secret Integration," *Saturday Evening Post*, 45 (19 and 26 December 1964), 37 ff.

12. James Dean Young, "The Enigma Variations of Thomas Pynchon," *Critique*, 10, No. 1 (Winter 1968), 72.

13. Raymond Olderman, *Beyond the Waste Land* (New Haven: Yale University Press, 1972), p. 131.

14. "Low-lands," *New World Writing*, 16 (1960), 85-108.

15. "Mortality and Mercy in Vienna," *Epoch*, 9, No. 4 (Spring 1959), 197-98.

16. "Entropy," *Kenyon Review*, 22, No. 2 (Spring 1960), 277-92.

17. Siegfried Kracauer, *From Caligari to Hitler* (1947; rpt. Princeton: Princeton University Press, 1971), p. 38.

18. Northrop Frye, *The Anatomy of Criticism* (1957: rpt. New York: Atheneum, 1966), pp. 308-12.

19. Edward Mendelson, "Gravity's Encyclopedia" in Levine and Leverenz, *Mindful Pleasures*, pp. 161-95.

20. Alvin P. Kernan, "A Theory of Satire," in *Satire: Modern Essays in Criticism*, ed. Ronald Paulson (Englewood Cliffs, N.J.: Prentice-Hall, 1971), p. 273.

21. Maynard Mack, "The Muse of Satire," in Paulson, *Satire*, p. 164.

22. Irving Feldman, "Keeping Cool," *Commentary*, 3, No. 36 (September 1963), 260.

23. Edward Mendelson, "Introduction," in *Pynchon: A Collection of Critical Essays* ed. Edward Mendelson (Englewood, N.J.: Prentice-Hall, 1978), p. 3.

24. Richard Patteson, "What Stencil Knew," *Critique*, 16, No. 2 (1974), 31-2.

25. Richard Poirier, "Rocket Power," *Saturday Review of the Arts*, 1, No. 3 (March 1973), 60.

26. John P. Leland, "Pynchon's Linguistic Demon," *Critique*, 16, No. 2 (1974), 49.

27. R. W. B. Lewis, *Trials of the Word* (New Haven: Yale University Press, 1965), p. 230.

28. Alan J. Friedman and Manfred Puetz, "Science as Metaphor: Thomas Pynchon and *Gravity's Rainbow*," *Contemporary Literature*, 15, No. 3 (Summer 1974), 347.

29. Tony Tanner, *City of Words*, p. 20. A good sample of the Prague Linguistic Circle's work appears in Paul Garvin, ed., *A Prague School Reader on Esthetics, Literary Structure and Style* (Washington, D.C.: Georgetown University Press, 1964).

30. Richard Poirier, *A World Elsewhere* (New York: Oxford University Press, 1966), p. 36.

31. Leo Spitzer, "Linguistic Perspectivism in the *Don Quixote*," in *Essays in Stylistic Analysis* ed. Howard S. Babb (New York: Harcourt, Brace Jovanovich, 1972), p. 167. This essay originally appeared in *Linguistics and Literary History*.

32. Lawrence C. Wolfley, "Repression's Rainbow: The Presence of Norman O. Brown in Pynchon's Big Novel," *PMLA*, 92, No. 5 (October 1977), 887.

33. Whitney Balliett, "Wha," *New Yorker*, 39, No. 17 (15 June 1963), 113.

34. John W. Hunt, "Comic Vision and Anti-Vision: The Novels of Joseph Heller and Thomas Pynchon" in *Adversity and Grace*, ed. Nathan A. Scott (Chicago: University of Chicago Press, 1968), p. 99.

35. Robert K. Morris, "Jumping Off the Golden Gate Bridge," *Nation*, 217, No. 2 (16 July 1973), p. 53.

36. Arnold Hauser, *The Social History of Art*, Volume IV (New York: Vintage Books, 1958), p. 236.

Chapter Two

1. Stephen Toulmin, *The Philosophy of Science* (1953; rpt. New York: Harper Torchbooks, 1960), p. 86.

2. Arthur Porter, *Cybernetics Simplified* (London: The English Universities Press, 1969), p. 29.

3. J. H. Briston and C.C. Gosselin, *Introduction to Plastics* (Feltham, England: Neunes Books, 1968) provides this and the following background information.

4. Norbert Wiener, *The Human Use of Human Beings* (1954; rpt. New York: Avon Books, 1967), p. 202.

5. Anne Mangel, "Maxwell's Demon, Entropy, Information: *The Crying of Lot 49*," *Triquarterly*, 20 (Winter 1971), 194-208.

6. "Journey into the Mind of Watts," *New York Times*, 12 June 1966. Reprinted in *Man Against Poverty* ed. Arthur I. Blaustein and Roger R. Woock (New York: Random House, 1968), pp. 146-58.

7. John H. Wellington, *South West Africa and Its Human Problems* (Oxford: The Clarendon Press, 1967), p. 148. Wellington quotes from another book.

8. Joseph Slade, "Escaping Rationalization: Options for the Self in *Gravity's Rainbow*," *Critique*, 18, No. 3 (April 1977), 31.

9. Edward Mendelson, "Pynchon's Gravity," *Yale Review*, 63, No. 4 (Summer 1973), 624-31.

10. Lance Ozier, "Antipointsman/Antimexico: Some Mathematical Imagery in *Gravity's Rainbow*," *Critique*, 16, No. 2 (1974), 81.

11. Jeremy Bernstein, *Einstein* (New York: Viking Press, 1973), p. 30.

12. Erwin Schrödinger, "Indeterminism in Physics," in *Great Ideas in Modern Science* ed. Robert Marks (New York: Bantam Books, 1967), p. 218.

13. A detailed contrast between deterministic and statistical analysis is Ozier's "Antipointman/Antimexico." Friedman and Puetz also make an incisive contrast (pp. 349-54).

14. Norbert Wiener, *Cybernetics* (New York: John Wiley and Sons, 1948), p. 56.

15. Robert W. Marks, "The Physical Aspects of Mind," in *Great Ideas in Modern Science*, p. 218.

16. Lance Ozier, "The Calculus of Transformation: More Mathematical Imagery in *Gravity's Rainbow*," *Twentieth Century Literature*, 21, No. 2 (May 1975), 193-210.

Chapter Three

1. Richard Poirier, "Embattled Underground," *New York Times Book Review*, 1 May 1966, p. 5.

2. George L. Mosse, *The Crisis of German Ideology* (New York: Oxford University Press, 1971), p. 24.

3. Richard Poirier, *The Performing Self* (New York: Oxford University Press, 1971), p. 24.

4. James Strachey, Anna Freud, Alix Strachey, and Alan Tyson eds. *The Complete Psychological Works of Sigmund Freud* (London: Hogarth Press, 1954), XIII, 73.

5. Ibid., VI, 255.

6. Ibid., III, 183.

7. Erik Erikson, *Young Man Luther* (1958; rpt. New York: W. W. Norton, 1962).

8. Norman O. Brown, *Life Against Death* (1959; rpt. Middletown, Conn.: Wesleyan University Press, 1970).

9. Wolfgang Köhler, *Gestalt Psychology* (1947; rpt. New York: Liveright, 1970), p. 103.

Chapter Four

1. My information about Malta comes from Brian Blouet, *A Short History of Malta* (New York: Frederick A. Praeger, 1967).

2. My source on this topic is John H. Wellington, *South West Africa and Its Human Issues* (Oxford: The Clarendon Press, 1967).

3. The following account depends on Wernher von Braun and Frederick I. Ordway, III, *History of Rocketry and Space Travel* (New York: Thomas Y. Crowell Company, 1966). My sources of information on British and American attempts to discover German rocket secrets are David Irving, *The Mare's Nest* (Boston: Little, Brown and Company, 1964) and James McGovern, *Crossbow and Overcast* (New York: William Morrow and Company, 1964).

4. This information on Thurn and Taxis comes from Laurin Zilliancus, *From Pillar to Post* (London: William Heinemann, Ltd., 1956).

5. Manfred Puetz, "Thomas Pynchon's *The Crying of Lot 49*," *Mosaic*, 7, No. 4 (Summer 1974), 131-32.

6. Richard Wasson, "Notes on a New Sensibility," *Partisan Review*, 36, No. 3 (Winter 1969), 474.

Chapter Five

1. James Nohrnberg, "Pynchon's Paraclete" in Mendelson, *Pynchon: A Collection of Critical Essays*, pp. 147-61.

2. Joseph Fahy, "Thomas Pynchon's *V*. and Mythology," *Critique*, 18, No. 3 (April 1977), 5-18.

3. Joseph Krafft, " 'And how Far-Fallen': Puritan Themes in *Gravity's Rainbow*," *Critique*, 18, No. 3 (April 1977), 62.

4. Joseph W. Slade, "Escaping Rationalization," p. 29.

5. A useful account of this tradition appears in Stephen F. Mason, *A History of the Sciences* (New York: Collier Books, 1962).

6. Arthur Edward Waite, *The Pictorial Key to the Tarot* (Blauvelt, N.Y.: Rudolf Steiner Publications, 1971).

7. Edward Mendelson, "Pynchon's Gravity," *The Yale Review*, 62, No. 4 (Summer 1973), 629.

Chapter Six

1. Siegfried Kracauer, *From Caligari to Hitler* (1947, rpt. Princeton University Press, 1971).

2. Peter Bogdanovich, *Fritz Lang in America* (London: Studio Vista Unlimited, 1967).

3. Paul M. Jensen, *The Cinema of Fritz Lang* (New York: A.S. Barnes and Company, 1969).
4. Carlos Alberto Astiz, "Introduction," José Hernandez, *Martin Fierro* (Albany: State University of New York Press, 1967), xiii.

Chapter Seven

1. Joseph W. Slade in *Thomas Pynchon*, pp. 81 ff. analyzes Pynchon's anti-romanticism.
2. M. D. Herter Norton, trans., *The Notebooks of Malte Laurids Brigge* (1949; rpt. New York: W. W. Norton, 1964), p. 77.
3. J. B. Leishman and Stephen Spender, trans., *Duino Elegies* (1939; rpt. New York: W. W. Norton, 1963), p. 122.
4. M. D. Herter Norton, trans., *Sonnets to Orpheus* (1942; rpt. New York: W. W. Norton, 1962), p. 121.
5. Alain Robbe-Grillet, *For a New Novel* (1963; rpt. New York: Grove Press, 1965), p. 140.
6. John Barth, *Chimera* (New York: Random House, 1972), p. 308.
7. Edward Mendelson, "Introduction," *Pynchon: A Collection of Critical Essays*.
8. David Crowart, "Pynchon's *The Crying of Lot 49* and the Paintings of Remedios Varo," *Critique*, 18, No. 3 (April 1977), 19-25.

Conclusion

1. Frank Kermode, *The Sense of an Ending* (London: Oxford University Press, 1967), p. 124.
2. Robert Jay Lifton, "Protean Man," *Partisan Review*, 35, No. 1 (Winter, 1968), 13-27.

INDEX